The Light in My Mind

by Joyce Passmore

"The Light in My Mind"
Copyright © Joyce Passmore, 2010
The moral right of the author has been asserted.

Cataloguing in Publication Data: a catalogue record
for this book is available from the British Library.

ISBN 978-0-9549772-5-2

Printed and Bound in England by
Character Graphics, Taunton, Somerset

Acknowledgements

Doctor Anna Knight

Staff of Holly Court, Yeovil

All Members of Yeovil Community Church,
"The Gateway", Yeovil

Simon Heyes (Development Officer and
        Company Secretary, Speak Up Somerset)

Norman Webley (Chairman, Speak Up Somerset)

Stephanus Kotze (Book Cover Graphics)

Character Graphics, Taunton

About The Author

The title of my book is based on a promise I made to myself when my life in the mental institution looked so black and impossible. I painted a picture, the whole page was black except for a small ball of yellow in the top right hand corner. The yellow represented my hope that one day the light would completely obliterate the blackness of my life for good and I would know the light and freedom I intended to have.

I have now reached the point where the blackness has been obliterated. This is why I named my book 'The Light in my Mind'. I do hope you enjoy reading it.

Joyce Passmore

Contents

Foreword

"Joyce is a survivor. She was incarcerated in Tone Vale Hospital near Taunton, Somerset. This was part of the failed Victorian experiment to look after what they called 'lunatics' in asylums, located in the countryside, well away from normal communities of town or village. Although well meaning in intent, these institutions were harsh, hostile and often violent, with doctors and nurses capable of inflicting severe punishments, both physical and emotional on their patients.

Joyce endured these conditions from the age of 13 until she was liberated from Tone Vale aged 28 in 1972. She moved to a Christian Rehabilitation home in Kent and then in 1979 returned to her native town, Yeovil, Somerset, where she lived in a bed-sit. During this year, at a meeting of professionals which Joyce attended, it was stated that her whole life has been taken away from her due to medical neglect. In 1983 she moved into a non-staffed supported housing project for people with long term mental health problems. By then, enlightened professionals realised that the conditions in these old hospitals were not conducive for rehabilitating patients and these institutions were unable to prepare patients to reintegrate into normal community life.

Joyce gradually regained some semblance of who she was and what she wanted to do with the rest of her life and in 1987 she moved into her own home, rented from the council. However she was still taking significant amounts of medication and receiving help from many professionals in Yeovil. Steve Denner, Consultant Psychologist, gave

7

her many hours of one to one support and then latterly Dr Anna Knight, Consultant Psychiatrist, continued this support and gradually helped her reduce the amount of medication she was taking. It was only in 2004, when aged 60, that she felt emotionally strong enough to say to herself 'enough is enough, I do not want or need this network of professional support any longer.'

Joyce finally stopped all her medication and planned her discharge, and as she elegantly said "I decided to retire from the service." She was helped in this process by Dr Anna Knight (Consultant Psychiatrist), Stephanie Bailey (Social Worker), Kay Turbull (Community Psychiatric Nurse), and Kate Jones (Community Support Worker). She can now relate her story of how she lost so much of her life to the psychiatric system which wittingly and unwittingly, colluded in preventing her from gaining a real sense of herself.

She returned to Tone Vale once it was closed, in order to convince herself that it no longer existed, but was distressed to see some of the roads on the new housing estate, named after doctors and nurses who had abused her and other patients when she was an inpatient.

Despite the loss of so much of her life, Joyce forgives those who may have inadvertently been involved in her being trapped in the psychiatric system for so long. Joyce looks forward to peaceful and fulfilling years ahead.

Chris Chambers. M.B.E. –
Senior Social Worker

Tributes To Faith And Fortitude

I have known Joyce Passmore for many years now and have been blessed by her gentle spirit in the midst of difficult times. Once she had committed her life to Christ, this amazing mix of faith and fortitude has seen her through a maze of the mundane and the miraculous.

I feel humbled to have been a small part of this wonderful journey from despair to deliverance, from hell to heaven. It will certainly be a book worth reading and will bring hope and joy to many people.

Congratulations Joyce and may the Lord continue His work in you.

Christian love
Godfrey Fearn (Rev.)

66 Joyce is a remarkable woman. She is a real survivor of Psychiatry and shows us professionals that sometimes the best that we can do for our patients is to liberate them from our services."

Doctor Anna Knight
(Consultant Psychiatrist)

"The Light in my Mind is a first-class personal story of recovery. On a wider scale it addresses the real public importance of how people diagnosed with mental health problems have been, and still are treated in our society. It is an account free of self-pity and essential reading for everyone who wants to know about the reality of mental health."

Simon Heyes – Speak Up Somerset

"We have been privileged to be Joyce's friends for over twenty years. In all that time we have seen her grow spiritually and in confidence to the level she is today."

Denis Stebbings and Yvonne Stebbings

"Joyce has always been there for me and my family. No one could ask for a more reliable and supportive friend."

Michelle Kotze

Joyce Passmore

"In our own journeys throughout our lives, we all encounter different types of challenges and are faced with many obstacles. Some of us, for one reason or another, find we cannot cope and need professional help. Others can be misunderstood and in some cases misdiagnosed. Even today there is a huge stigma and ignorance surrounding mental health issues. Doctors' surgeries around the country do not have the time, or knowledge to treat the early signs associated with poor mental health. This often means having to resort to drugs, which then leads to long term dependency. Five years ago I was very fortunate to meet Joyce Passmore, a woman whom although dealt many a bad hand in life, showed a remarkable optimism, resilience and an infectious positive attitude. I do not want to talk about Joyce's history I would rather focus on how she rose above the stigma and injustices that weaved their way through her life. She is an intelligent woman, understanding her problems often with more accuracy than any professional and usually helping others on the way. I do not want to patronise Joyce, but rather celebrate the inspiration she has on others, breaking down the walls of misunderstanding surrounding mental health issues. An accomplished poet Joyce's words have brought comfort to many at their lowest, sometimes helping them in putting their lives in perspective. This brings me to the story of Joyce's life. It is an inspiring work which reaches into what makes us who we are, and how the vulnerable are often stigmatised. This first-hand insight is invaluable to everyone. It will change the way you think and feel about humanity. Thank you Joyce.

Chris Clark (M.I.N.T.)

1

Forgotten Dreams

Each year I watch *White Christmas* (1954), a film with Bing Crosby, Danny Kaye, Vera Ellen and Rosemary Clooney. It is one of the joys I have every Christmas. I see the children dressed in their crinoline styled dresses sing with happy faces around a Christmas tree. In their eyes I see the dreams of all children. Childhood is the most magical time of our lives, everything seems possible. It is also the shortest, adult life arrives almost without warning. We brace ourselves against the struggle that follows, drawing comfort from the gossamer of our childhood. I must have had similar dreams as a child, only I cannot remember them. This brought some sadness into my life in the subsequent years. Fifteen years on prescription drugs in a mental hospital from the age of thirteen deleted my childhood.

In the early years I constructed an approximation of what I might have wished for as a child. I marry a wonderful man who loves me dearly. I wear a crinoline dress of white satin at my wedding, and hold a bouquet of deep red roses that trail down entwined by small delicate green leaves. A tiara sparkles on my head and the sun shining on the tiara makes it even more radiant. Six bridesmaids in red velvet dresses have white fluffy muffs with red and white small rose buds in their hair. They carry the train of my wedding dress as I walk down the aisle of the church to make my wedding vows. The scene changes to a dinner table. I sit with my husband and the children we have raised together. I have just finished cooking and with the plates in front of us, we are ready to

13

eat. I can imagine there may have been times when I would have to remind the children not to speak with their mouth full. These are the events of an ordinary life and in my life never to be fulfilled. For me they are just forgotten dreams.

I was born on the 10th March 1944 at the former Yeovil maternity home. I have no idea what I weighed, but was given a clean bill of health by the medical staff. I was christened at Yeovil Trinity Church.

Many children have childhood illnesses and I was no exception. I suffered with sinus problems which the specialist felt could be helped by a small operation. His aim was to clear the sinuses. I was aged nine when I was admitted to Yeovil General Hospital for this operation. The surgeon decided when I was on the operating table to take out my tonsils and adenoids as well. This was without any parental permission. In the hospital after the operation I remember living on endless jelly and ice cream. When I returned home a friend came to visit me. As we were talking, with my mother present, I found I started to have a build-up of saliva in my mouth. I excused myself and went into the kitchen and spat it out. Not long afterwards I had to excuse myself again. The saliva had become discoloured. I said nothing until my friend left then I told my mother who could now see the discoloured saliva for herself. This started to happen at approximately 2.00 pm. My mother went to a nurse who lived nearby to see if this was normal. She was told by the nurse it was quite normal. The symptoms gradually got worse as the time passed, and I was feeling quite frightened. I realised I was now losing blood. I was nine and old enough to realise something was seriously wrong. As this became increasingly worse, my parents put me into their bed and surrounded me with white towels which were soon soaked with the blood I was losing. My blond hair was matted by it. It was now coming away in large clots which were described by my father as "looking like the insides of a rabbit."

I do not remember the doctor coming at around 2.00 am as I was unconscious. He immediately called for an ambulance and warned my parents I may not survive long enough to get to the hospital. I did. My lifeless body was saved by a transfusion. A nurse shared with my parents that another little girl nearly died through the same operation the week before, and by the same surgeon. The staff nicknamed him 'the butcher'. I later heard he was nearing retirement and having become a 'liability' in the eyes of the hospital, he was asked to leave early. I was kept in the acute ward with five other very sick children until I was well enough to go home.

This incident left me with recurring nightmares where I could see myself haemorrhaging and everything turning red, I would wake up in perspiration. This went on for a number of years but then ceased. I did have questions after this incident which I should have asked my parents at the time. They were difficult questions to ask and I knew they would cause pain however I tried to put them. Why was something not done sooner? Did they want me to live? Was I really wanted? These were the questions racing around in my young head. So much pain could have been avoided if I had asked. Instead they piled up inside me – the beginning of a mountain of doubts. In hindsight, I can see my mistake and would always advise people to ask for answers rather than let questions fester inside them. Mine was not a family that talked about those important things. I had things I wanted to talk about and not doing so was tearing me apart inwardly. No one would have known this, as like most children I showed a resilience against the inward pain I felt.

Many of my early years are a blank and hold just a few memories of the ordinary life of a child. I used to go to Saturday morning pictures with some friends. The Odeon Cinema organised a talent contest at the local Assembly Rooms for the children to take part. My friends dared me to enter as they knew I could sing. I took the dare and ended up by being one of the winners! I laugh as I remember the shock on my friends' faces. I also entered myself for a TV talent show where the auditions were held at the Manor Hotel in Yeovil. I sang a Ruby Murray song *"Goodbye Jimmy Goodbye"* in front of four judges and was given a favourable response and was going through to the next round. I can remember coming out of the audition into the room where other hopefuls and their parents were waiting. I was applauded by them and some lovely comments were made. I suddenly became aware that my father was standing at the back of the room looking very proud; I did not know he was going to be there.

One very important thing I did as a child was to attend Sunday School. I was sent, so that the Sunday dinner could be cooked in peace but I enjoyed going. I did play about at times like the other children, yet I heard about Jesus and how He loved me. His promises of never leaving me or forsaking me were so wonderful. When I sang of Jesus I felt that every word I was singing was to Him. It seemed at times it was just Jesus and me although the room was full of other people. Every Christmas, because I had blond hair and a good singing voice, I would be the Angel Gabriel in the Nativity play. Looking back at those times in the small Baptist Church it seemed that as the years continued, so my Angel Gabriel wings improved in quality and design. I did not know how important my Sunday School days were going to be. The teaching I was given was so vital for the impossible life I had ahead. Without the mustard seed of faith I had at that time, I would not be here to write this book today. I had no idea that an ordinary day of going to school was going to be the start of my life spiralling out of my control. I walked to school that day with my friends chattering and laughing as usual and nothing seemed amiss. The teacher took the register and the lesson started. I was always able to be near the top of the class with all the English subjects. I did struggle a bit with Maths and Geography, yet I loved school and managed to stay in the top stream. I was in a geography lesson listening to the teacher and started to find a tight band forming around my head. I had no idea what it was and asked to leave the classroom for some water, intending to go to the drinking tap in the nearby cloakroom. Everything started to feel strange and distant. I was found collapsed on the floor of the cloakroom; I had not reached the drinking tap. On waking I found I was in the school's first aid room with the headmistress who was also a state registered nurse, she said I had just had an epileptic fit. I could not fully take it in at the time, but when I did I was shocked. The staff wanted me to go home. My immediate reaction was, "No!" It was an answer that came straight out. I did not fully understand that reaction and I do not think the staff did either but they did let me go back to class. It was the start of more attacks and I kept insisting on my parents not being told anything and asking to go back to class. Looking back at that time and trying to make some sense of it, I asked myself "was it because of my unanswered questions when I had my haemorrhage?" I have no definite answers even now. It was a sad and confusing time for all concerned.

My life changed suddenly. In the past I represented the school in the high jump and hundred yards, which I usually won. Now I had to sit by a teacher, away from the other pupils in case I had an attack. I was no longer allowed to play with the other children at playtime in case I hurt myself. Eventually my parents had to be told of the attacks that had now risen to approximately five every day. This meant frequent visits to the General Practitioner. I was prescribed anti-convulsive medication yet the attacks continued. Looking back I could have been a target for bullies, we hear so much of it today. Yet I was never a subject of any bullying even though I was looked upon as different.

One domestic science lesson, the teacher asked us to bake a Christmas cake for our families. This was considered to be something "big" by the pupils. I prepared the mixture and greased the cake tin, spooned in the ingredients and placed it into the oven which I shared with another pupil. I had another attack and had to go to the first aid room. I had never been in this room until the attacks started and now it was getting to be very familiar. Once again, after I felt well enough I returned to class. I found that my cake had been forgotten and was burnt to a cinder. The pupil who was to watch it forgot because she was concentrating on her own. The domestic science teacher asked the other pupils if they had any spare ingredients. I can remember the whole class contributed. There were spoonfuls given from different pupils, dollops from others, which added up to enough for another cake to be made. The teacher mixed the ingredients and asked me to stir once and make a wish. I closed my eyes and silently wished for my life to be back to normal, and to be well. When I opened my eyes the other pupils had left their tables and surrounded mine. I could sense that they knew what my silent wish was and wished the same for me. The warmth on their faces as they smiled at me was so different from the heat of the ovens. It made me feel a glow inside. I remember this, as I was feeling low at the time and they had shown me kindness when I really needed it.

I had to see the doctor on a regular basis, but I was totally unaware that the visit with my mother on November 23rd 1957 was going to turn out the way it did. I can recall the details of this fateful day as if it happened yesterday. As I entered the doctor's surgery I noticed that one chair was placed right in front of him, the other chair that was usually beside it was by the door. The doctor ushered me to sit on the chair facing him. My mother was out of my vision sitting behind me by the door. The doctor smiled at me and he asked if I would consider going into hospital for three weeks for my medication to be sorted out. I started to turn to look at my mum for advice but the doctor drew my attention away from her, I wanted her help as this was a big decision. I was thirteen years old but I realised I had to make this decision. My mother remained silent. My immediate thought was a no, then I wondered if it would be worth it if in three weeks my life would be back to normal. I seemed to take ages with my thoughts tossing back and forth between the yes and no. I suddenly decided to say yes, which was not easy. The very next words that the doctor said remain very clear even to this day. He told me the hospital I had just said yes to, was to be the mental hospital in Taunton called Tone Vale. The shock was so bad that I cried out "No! You can't. I do not want to go. No!"

19

I had been totally misled by this pre-arranged charade. I discovered later that it had all been discussed previously without my knowledge. I had sealed my own fate by this awful deceit. Why did they ask me in the first place if they had already made up their minds? My trust in doctors diminished even more. I looked at my mother and in utter disbelief just shook my head at the way this was done. Inwardly I alienated myself from my family. I felt dead to life and those around me.

The damage done in the doctor's surgery that morning was compounded by the arrangements to take me to the hospital that afternoon. The trip to the hospital was in silence as I watched the sign-posts, showing I was getting nearer. I had lost all trust and felt physical pain as I struggled to keep control of my emotions. My hurt was overwhelming.

This was a sudden and unexpected change and I could not understand why no one had bothered to tell me anything or explain why this was happening.

2
Fear Into The Unknown

My admittance at such a young age remained a mystery until I started researching fifty years later. I found answers to many of my questions. While my parents were still alive, I never found the right moment to ask them for the answers I needed. I had a mountain of questions by now. I have tried to understand by putting myself in their shoes. Perhaps they believed that they had acted in good faith. Perhaps they struggled with the guilt of letting it happen. "Perhaps" was and still is pointless. It did not help in knowing what they thought.

Tone Vale delivered a life sentence. Even if I could remember the dreams I had as a child, those years in hospital determined a very different path for me, one littered with stigma, prejudice and ignorance. I know I am not alone in this as society shrinks from mental illness, and treats you like an outsider. I am one of the few who was eventually freed.

I met other children at Tone Vale who like me had never felt the innocent thrill of what life might hold. It fills me with sadness to think of them. That hospital cancelled out the promise of so many lives. I know from personal experience that children who are damaged in their early years can grow up to become damaged adults. The people I refer to in the book never made it out of hospital to full recovery. I could have suffered a similar fate but I never gave up and this is why my story is of hope.

Arriving at the hospital I was sent to the children's unit, ironically called "Merrifield." It was not merry and there were no fields for the children to play outside. I cannot remember any of us being allowed to play outside. I remember on arrival, still in silence, looking at the place from outside and saying to myself that this was a massive mistake, and it was. The inside of the children's wing looked cold and sparse. The large expanse of dark granite flooring was marked over the many years of being used. The cleaner worked hard to keep it clean, but really could make no impression on its appearance. There were chairs that surrounded the room and the other children who were much younger than me played as their capabilities would allow them. I sat on one of the chairs and became aware that the children were oblivious to their surroundings and to themselves – I could not understand their behaviour. It became apparent to me why this was happening the very next day after being admitted. I was being put on medications that I had not had before. This was in the day time, and that very same evening I was put on sleeping tablets! The sleeping tablets were not necessary but I had no choice. The day time medication had effects that caused me to be less aware of who and where I was. This is the only way it can be described, I then realised why the other children seemed unaware.

The old mental health system relied on the use of tranquillisers in abundance. The railings that surrounded the hospital were apparently taken down by a forward thinking doctor. It was not progress at all, as due to the massive usage of drugs each patient was locked into their own personal prison, unable to function normally. It was a downhill spiral.

Many of the children I met in "Merrifield" would be classed today as physically unwell. Some had deformities; another had water on the brain. Others would be recognised today as having learning difficulties. Yet it was the way the old mental health system worked. Anyone who seemed different or who did not fit in to what society classed as "normal" was shut away. To live here cost £42 and 15 shillings a week for each child. Victorian attitude was still in practice in the 1950s-1970s and the 18th century hospital was still dishing out harsh treatments. The regime seemed to be of punishment rather than of real constructive help. I had been alienated from my family and my friends and had no idea what my relations knew or did not know. In fact I felt abandoned with so much hurt bursting inside me. I looked around me and just felt devastated by this chain of events. I kept saying to myself that I would be leaving in three weeks as the doctors promised. I saw each day through with the aim of surviving this ordeal for the three weeks and then returning home.

During this time the attacks were still happening and I was sent to Guys Hospital in London to see a Neurologist and have brain scans. My research fifty years later led me to discover these letters written by Guys Hospital to the doctor in Tone Vale:-

1. The brain scan is grossly abnormal with much paroxysmal general slow activity and a more distinct and persistent theta focus in the right temporal region. It produced bursts of generalized slow waves and multiple spiky waves, constituting a convulsive response. The records suggests epileptic instability with probably a right temporal epileptic focus.

Another letter was sent around the same time.

2. I write rather urgently to put you in the picture over Joyce Passmore. Her EEG confirmed her epilepsy when she was seen by the Neurologist at Guys Hospital. We had great difficulties in controlling her attacks. First we tried Epanutin with Mysoline and Phenobarbitone. She was subsequently changed to Mysoline 250 mgs (tds) (3 times a day). Nydrane 1 tablet (tds). Phenobarbitone half a grain (td) twice a day. Librium 2 tablets (td) She is now free from her attacks.

Imagine my feelings on discovering proof that not only had I been sent to a mental hospital for a physical disability, but also that medication had been prescribed which had stopped the epileptic attacks! There was actually no reason why I should not have been discharged. Guys Hospital said it would be the best thing for me. I continued my research and found that only one of the four prescribed tablets was continued after returning to Tone Vale. As a result the attacks started again. It was discovered that I had a scar on the brain. Another discovery was that I had cranial nerve damage. This all helped answer my questions when other signs of illness arose that I could not explain at the time.

Everything was happening so fast. It was like a hurricane over which I had no control. It was impossible to focus on my faith in Jesus at that time. All I knew was that I wanted to get home and still believed that this would happen. Why were these people being so inhuman? The doctor would come to the children's wing daily and I would ask him about the arrangements to go home.

I am sure doctors in the psychiatric field had courses on how to talk to patients but never really saying anything! I could not have been more direct when asking him about going home. There was never an answer to my questions. I spent so long in hope and expectancy, and expended so much energy in my quest to go home.

Being a grown up and not being told what is going to happen to you is bad enough. A child being in that same position can be totally destroyed. There is no way it can be dressed up to sound better. As I began to feel the utter hopelessness of my situation I realised how much I needed Jesus. My trust in people had been scrambled to bits in every way by the tremendous hurt they had inflicted.

3
Where Are You?

I had lost touch with the outside world and my friends were people that I never saw or knew any more. School friends, whom I met forty years later, summed it up correctly when they said "What happened to you? You just disappeared." It was true, I was with them one day and then they lost sight of me for the next forty years. As far as they were concerned I was never mentioned and did not exist. Relatives alive today were never aware of what happened and still are not. They have families now who do not know of my existence. The every day happenings I would have been involved in did not apply to me any more.

It began to dawn on me in the midst of the havoc of my life, that God was the only one who would listen to me. I began to pray more. The medication hazed a lot of my life, yet nothing stopped me from realising my need of the Lord. I started to recognise my love for Him. St Luke's Church, in the grounds of Tone Vale Hospital, offered a life saving route to God. I did not benefit much from the Sunday services in the chapel because the other patients were disturbed and noisy. It was hard to hear what the Lord was saying to me personally so I asked permission to go to the church on my own and was allowed 15 minutes each day. In the church I poured out to Him my worries, fears, my confusion, my hurts and my longings. Words I had learned in Sunday School became my strength every day. Whenever I felt low or in utter despair, these words would come to me "I will never leave you or forsake you." I whispered "Thank you Jesus."

The wonderful knowledge of His love became very real. It was the medicine I needed to give me the will to carry on. Visiting the church I would run, taking the shortest route, so I could make every second count. I sat on the pew nearest the door by an ancient mosaic on the wall to save time. Day in, day out for more than ten years, I bowed my head and asked the Lord for help, my hands were clasped so tightly at times that my knuckles became red. Those brief fifteen minutes were so important and hardly long enough for me at times. As months turned to years, I became bolder when I prayed. In times of doubt I would remind Him that I was there. I knew He was my Heavenly Father and I also knew that however my prayers poured out He would understand. I knew for certain that He was never going to turn away and see me as a lost cause. He loved me then, and His love for me continues to this day. My love for Him has increased so much from the mustard seed of faith I first had.

Fortunately, a member of staff never caught me pouring my heart out, that would have meant more injections, more tranquillizers and more numbness. I always felt uplifted after my times in the hospital church. I could talk to the Lord in confidence without fear of repercussion whereas if I shared my innermost thoughts with a member of the medical staff, I risked being given more treatment.

I was transferred to the main hospital when I was sixteen. The years had started to mount. Though it was called a hospital the last thing that one could do was to share how you felt. I did have all sorts of emotions that I had to keep hidden. It became more intimidating as I was now with adults and some were very unwell. The whole place oozed with despair, a hidden world that many did not realise existed.

The epilepsy, which had been classed as 'childhood epilepsy', had stopped but it was not considered that I should go home. I never saw many people discharged, but I always knew from day one that I should not have been placed there. No one seemed to understand that I wanted my life back! I kept asking to leave, their answer was even more medication to keep me calm. Each patient had to be sufficiently sedated so the staff could have total control. It was a cruel and archaic way to treat people. I began to be aware of the plight of other patients with serious mental health problems. I could see their suffering and also the constant injustice from some of those who treated us. Even at my young age I empathised with them and yearned with real passion that they, as well as myself could be well and out of that place.

In the time I spent in the church, as I shared every single thought and feeling with my Heavenly Father, I would also pray for the other patients. I found it hard to pray for the staff, though I realise now that this is what God asks of us.

I did not know at that time Tone Vale was to be my home for fifteen years. My future was to be decided by other people. I was there to be talked about but not talked to. Decisions were made for me and implemented; I would be whisked off for new treatments with no warning or explanation. I had no voice! My identity was destroyed. I was being institutionalised although I did not recognise it. I was being forced to submit to their way of life and get sucked into a world where I did not belong, but I knew it was important not to let the system take me over completely. I was never a person to cause trouble, but I had a quiet determination that some part of me would stay "me" in all that was happening to me. I believe my faith enabled me to do this. I was expected to give in to this bizarre way of life, yet with Jesus I had this wonderful extra strength, which at times saw me through impossible situations. It was like having my own steel security box inside me, which only the Lord and I were aware of. In it was our determination to stay the course and see it through whatever it took.

One thing I did do in the hospital was write poetry; I always had a pen and paper handy. Often if I could not sleep or the daily pressures mounted up, the words would flow out in rhyme – and always to Jesus, the Author and Finisher of my faith. I used to write Christian poetry, usually submitting four each month in the hospital magazine, copies were sent to every ward. I could see patients locked in their own terrifying worlds and yet the Lord broke the barrier for one patient and my poetry played a part. One day, as I was walking up the long corridor, which was noisy and busy with patients and staff, a voice boomed out above the rest. "Hey! Aren't you the one who loves God?" I looked round and saw two nurses escorting a lady who looked very disturbed. She was looking at me and I was surprised to find her talking to me but called back to her "Yes, and He loves you too." The expressions on the nurses' faces registered shock and disapproval! This lady could never normally put an intelligible sentence together. Her indication that she knew I loved God led the staff to discover that she could read my poetry. Not only that, but that she could also write! All her life she had been judged by the way she appeared and acted; no one had bothered to find out what she could or could not do. She was discarded by society and was looked upon as a waste of time. She read a poem of mine to the staff and it opened new doors for her. For the first time, I felt real joy as I learned the valuable lesson that the outward appearance does not reflect the person inside – a lesson we all need to take heed of.

4
Lost?

It is hard to recollect exact times of the wards I was put on and at what age; I was shuttled from one place to another. The years of my life melded into the world in which I was forced to live. Time and age, birthdays and Christmas ceased to have any significance. The first adult ward I stayed on was at the front of the hospital and called Mary Ward, it looked onto the car park. As weeks and months turned into years, the authorities in charge moved me in stages to the back of the hospital. Out of sight – out of mind? The first ward I was admitted to in the main hospital was, I feel, to introduce me to this new experience so I could be eased into far worse. This is exactly what happened.

On Mary ward there was a doctor, who as part of his training to be a general practitioner, was seeking to widen his experience by working in the mental health system. He had a great understanding and a caring manner. He came to me one day and said that he felt I needed a break from the ward. Oh boy, how right he was! He asked a nurse, and her friend who worked in the canteen, if they would be willing to take me into Taunton. It was arranged. The staff and I went to British Home Stores to have a cake and a cup of tea. As we sat there, they talked about the things connected with their lives and I quietly drank my tea and ate my cake from pink crockery, which British Homes Stores provided. I had nothing to share or say. When it came time to go, I was shocked to see the two members of staff slip the plates, cups and saucers into their bags and trying to make me do the same. I may have been drugged to the hilt, but I knew they were trying to make me steal. I said "No that is stealing and I do not steal." They knew time was limited in case they got caught so they tried to persuade me again. They got a definite "No" again. They had the stolen crockery with them but I did not. Leaving British Home Stores they decided to go to the house of one of the girls and the mother went to the kitchen. I was looking on and feeling very unhappy about their stealing. The mother opened a cupboard in her kitchen and it was nearly full of the pink British Home Stores crockery. The staff added their stolen goods to it while I remained silent, feeling shock and disgust. I was then warned not to say anything to anyone at the hospital. On my return to the hospital I told no one because I was scared, but I felt angry inside. I knew I was better than that. A few weeks later, the same well meaning GP suggested that I should go into Taunton again. He said he would arrange for me to go with the same two staff. I said no thank you. Shocked by my response, he tried to persuade me that the outing would do me good, but inwardly I knew it would do the opposite. When I kept refusing his offer, he started to become impatient, which hurt as he had been the only person that had shown me any real kindness since I had been admitted to the hospital. He asked my father to come to the ward to try and persuade me. I was sitting in the office where the two of them kept pressurising me. I knew the tears I had carried inside me for so long were going to erupt. I suddenly reached breaking point and blurted out at the same time "I cannot, they stole some things." The doctor was very understanding and let the tears come until there were no more to shed. My father stayed silent. It was only then that the doctor asked me the details. It was hard in one sense but an almighty relief in another. It was no longer a fear I had to hold in any more.

The doctor said he would need to report this incident to the Matron. She interviewed the two members of staff concerned. They both admitted to stealing and trying to make me do the same. They were both sacked. It was not easy to feel I had been responsible for them losing their jobs however I was not ashamed that I stood by my decision not to steal for them. I later heard that they had joined the army. I was pleased and shocked to hear that. They certainly needed discipline and guidelines in their lives and the army would definitely give it to them. Perhaps I did them a favour in a roundabout way!

After this experience I was not asked to go anywhere else. This was a learning experience for all concerned. Sadly it was found to be a regular problem where some staff stole from the patients. It was only a few years later I had a sheepskin coat stolen which only the staff had access to. The day it was found missing by the ward sister, she informed the police. Two officers came to see me as they had been called to the hospital, and I asked "Do you know there is a big problem with staff stealing from the patients?" They were really kind and said they were very aware as they have had been called to the hospital many times before. They admitted that it was almost impossible to ever trace the stolen goods. They felt for those of us who were taken advantage of in this way but I never saw my coat again.

I used to pray about my life with its hurts and fears. When the same feelings returned I would pray again. I did not grasp that when I prayed and left them at the Cross of Jesus I should have left them there. I kept taking them back and praying about them all over again. I was not aware as I am now of the awesome power of Jesus and His promises. I was constantly asking the staff to let me leave but only felt utter hopelessness when asking them. I never stopped believing that Jesus was listening and was going to sort it out. I became very depressed by being left in the hospital for so long. I had shown no signs of depression on entering, but this now became my illness. Depression is a most debilitating illness that receives an unsympathetic press because it cannot be seen, the assumption being that it is all in the mind. The antidote that is often offered is "pull yourself together." Depression is in the mind but it is very real. It can be caused by a chemical imbalance in the brain and depression can paralyse your ability to function. I suffered with this and if I could have "snapped out of the depression" I would have been the first to have wanted to do it. I saw my life as a hopeless waste of time. The thought would consume me one day and the next and the one after that. There seemed no end to the misery. It is difficult to describe, but imagine thousands of extremely thin wires scrambled together. Each one of those thin wires is transmitting terrible thoughts and going at full pelt. "You have no purpose; you're a waste of time; you have nothing in you of any use; you just take up space; no one wants you; no one loves you." These are only a few of the terrible thoughts you may have. There is no stopping them. There can be thousands, and everyone who suffers has their own individual torment. Put that tangled mess inside your head, now try and function. It is impossible. There were times I used to hold my head and cry out "Please stop!" But it continued day and night. It is the loneliest illness on earth, no-one wants to know someone suffering from depression and people avoid you. If I wore a bandage on my head, people would approach me offering sympathy and ask what was wrong. If I told them I wore the bandage because of the pain and torment inside my head, how would they react?

Depression does not require a bandage but it deserves the same sympathy. A kind word from a friend, who is prepared to listen as well, does wonders for the spirit. When clinical depression invades a person's life and they are suffering badly they need help in so many ways. It is a time where your support and being there will not always be easy, yet the rewards can be so great when the person is well. When the help and understanding does not come, the imaginary wires with all the tormenting thoughts and despair, may bring about the need for hospital care either as an in or out patient. The medication begins and then comes the reliance on it. After a long period of being on medication it loses its effectiveness. When someone is in this situation, where hope and rational thinking are paralysed, it seems impossible to achieve quietness of mind, their thinking becomes distorted. They can no longer rationalise their thoughts, and for some, the only way to achieve the peace they crave is suicide. Some would say this is a coward's way out or that it is selfish, but to the person in this situation it sadly seems to be the only way.

I too have reached the point where rational thoughts disappear. For six years all I wanted was a permanent solution to the hell I was living in and by rights I should not be alive. I thank God so much that I am alive today. By His grace, even when life gets tough I do not ever think of ending my life.

No words can express how thrilled I am to have my life back, renewed and refreshed. He helped me realise I had worth and if I did not know this, then I would not be able to write this book. Someone reading this could be going through depression and feel they are not worth anything.

Never give in to that way of thinking. Depression robs you of seeing how much God loves you. You are loved and you are vital and essential to have and to know. Never give up, and never give in.

There needs to be a greater understanding of this illness. Do you shy away from sufferers with depression? Can you stand by and let them descend into hopelessness? A few moments of your time, a listening ear, a chance to unload, can help to stop the driving force within them. Just to know that there is someone who cares can halt the feelings of worthlessness. We all need that kind of reassurance whether we suffer with depression or not.

Depression is a real illness and has no respect for who you are at all. Whatever your standing in life, however much money you may have, however strong you may seem, unexpected circumstances can throw you off balance. People who suffer from this illness are reluctant to share how they feel for fear of rejection. Put yourself in the same situation as such people, would you want to be avoided and made to feel you were not wanted?

Sometimes good can come from facing those who ridicule your mental health state. I had to have an operation in a General Hospital. This was very hard for me knowing that some of the staff in general hospitals are not equipped in understanding those who have mental health needs. This leads to more suffering for patients. Waiting with the other patients who were due surgery that day a young doctor in his white coat came in and sat down with a nurse and looked through the different notes of those of us who were waiting.

They came to my notes as I recognised some bright yellow paper that it had in them. True to form the doctor and nurse were pointing at my notes and giggled. As they continued in this way for some time I walked up to them calmly and said "I see you are laughing at my medical notes, can I help by explaining my notes to you?" They were both shocked and embarrassed to find me there as I waited calmly for them to answer. The young doctor said "Go and sit down and I will see you in a moment." I replied calmly "Thank you very much I would appreciate that," and I went and sat down. The laughter stopped and the nurses who were sat the other side of the table glanced at each other and carried on with their work. The doctor was the anaesthetist and he called me into his room to discuss my operation. He had my notes with him and looked at my medical history as we discussed the epidural I was to have for my operation. In my notes it had some of my mental health history and as he asked me about this I was quite honest and open with my answers. I said I had suffered with depression as he asked more questions. I said I asked for an epidural in order to make sure I could leave the hospital the next day. I noticed how he was looking me in a quizzical fashion as I spoke. I did not know what to feel when he suddenly said "You are quite sensible aren't you?" His innocent ignorance was unbelievable. I said light heartedly "Just because I have suffered with a psychiatric illness does not mean that everything I say or do is rubbish or not to be believed." I said in a part joking manner that "I was quite sensible enough to come over and point out that my notes are not to be laughed at. I feel I have suffered enough and do not deserve it." I stayed calm and polite but felt this point needed to be made. He suddenly looked at me and said "I was laughing at your notes Miss Passmore and I do apologise to you for doing that. I hope you can forgive me." He was being genuine and I said "Thank you for apologising as it means a great deal to me, many do not." His lack of knowledge over anything to do with the mentally ill was astounding to me. I went on answering more of his questions about the mentally unwell, as he was genuinely interested. I then said to him "Doctor, you are young enough to make a change in this hospital where the mentally unwell are concerned. They deserve respect and if you can help bring this about then this has all been worthwhile." He got hold of my hand and shook it saying it had been a real privilege to meet me. This doctor went up in my estimation big time. He was honest enough to admit that he had been laughing at my medical notes. He had his eyes opened and he was not too proud to say sorry. This was all that was necessary. The nurse who had been laughing with him said flippantly "We were not laughing at your notes." I could have told her to go and see the doctor that I had just spoken to, but realised this problem will continue until the nursing bodies in General and Mental hospitals meet to discuss how to stop it from happening. I now had to prepare for the operation I was there for. I knew in my heart that a very valuable lesson was taken on board that day and I felt so pleased. The doctor was very caring as I laid awake whilst my operation was taking place.

Sadly I could write a volume of people's accounts when entering a general hospital, but it would be too painful to write. This is a problem that has existed for far to long and needs to be addressed.

I left the next morning by 9am. The surgeon came to see if the operation was successful and the orthopaedic technician arrived soon afterwards with my crutches and special boot. As soon as he was happy I was on the phone to my friend asking for her to come and collect me as we arranged. Others on the ward could not understand why my leaving went so smoothly. They said that they were wanting to leave and could not. I said when you are well enough you need to say what you are wanting sometimes. I did not want to go in to my circumstances. Leaving the hospital was my priority now.

Some General Practitioners recognise this is a problem and some do not. The psychiatric staff do. This needs to be recognised by all because it can be a life threatening problem. Writing articles on mental health issues for a magazine I named one "Mental or Physical Illness?" I stated the problems that exist and I had many replies back thanking me for highlighting this problem. One phone call summed up everything this problem causes. A social worker thanked me for writing the article and told me that one of her patients was not feeling at all well physically. She was taken to the general hospital by the social worker. Her mental health history was of more interest to the nursing staff in the accident and emergency unit and she was sent home with no treatment. Sadly she was found unconscious and collapsed on the floor of her home the next day. She had to be rushed to hospital and needed emergency surgery to save her life. People who suffer with psychiatric illness are not exempt from physical illnesses.

Many things happened on Mary Ward and one of those was of the ward psychiatrist continuing to prescribe more and more drugs for me. He would not stop any previous tablets even though the sister mentioned her concerns to him. I swallowed the ever increasing amounts he was prescribing and I became so ill that I eventually lost the use of my limbs.

Detached from the outside world, I lay in bed staring into space; I cannot even remember being fed. Eventually, the ward sister phoned my parents to express her concern for my health. My father came to see the sister, who told him what was happening. He went to see the deputy matron, a fair but no-nonsense woman, who came to see for herself. When she saw the state I was in, she relieved the psychiatrist of his duties immediately. Whatever happened after this I do not know. I never saw him on the ward again and the medication was stopped immediately. My system had been badly poisoned by the amount of medication this doctor was making me have – I dare not think what his motives were. He was told by the sister and yet he did not stop. How far was he prepared to go? To speed up my recovery, the hospital let my parents take me to Minehead every day to breathe in the sea air. They had to drag me along the seafront and my legs dangled beneath me like a puppet's. A woman once asked them what was the matter, my parents felt embarrassed and with difficulty said that I had been poisoned by medication. When they could not drag me any further, we used to sit on the sea wall and stare at the ocean. Then we would have another go at trying to walk. This went on for days until the use of my legs came back.

How do you come to terms with a near death experience that should never have happened? I know the ward sister risked her job to save my life, I will always be grateful for her care at this time. I gave her my thanks, at least there were some 'good-uns' around!

I was an avid reader of Agatha Christie mystery books; they helped me escape from my own terrible life. One evening I had reached the last two chapters of the book I was reading. The lights were usually shut off at 6.30 pm and I asked a nurse if I could have some light to finish my book. She brought one of the night lamps used by the night nurses. Having been put into bed because I had an injured back I had to place the lamp on my shoulder in order to read. The lamp was a metal nine inch lamp and about four inches square; the light bulb itself was in the top part of the lamp. I started to read but fell asleep before I had finished, and while I slept the night nurse had taken the lamp away. I awoke in terrible pain; I felt my body was on fire. I cried out to the nurses but they were busy on the other side of the ward. Restricted by cot sides and injured back, I managed to slide down and out of the bed and I struggled to get to where the nurses were. I could not understand what was happening to me but I knew something was dreadfully wrong, I was yelling with the pain. One of the nurses noticed immediately that the skin on the top part of my body was very inflamed. She licked her finger, placed it on the inflammation and then put it to her mouth. "Acid, she has acid on her skin!" was what I heard from her. They acted very promptly and called the resident GP (the one who had been so kind to me). He found that I had been badly burned by acid from the lamp. The nurse remembered that the lamp was out when she took it from my shoulder. A great deal of treatment took place that night and then I was heavily bandaged. It was an awful experience. The next day the hospital management committee, the Matron and the nurses who were present when this happened all invaded the ward. I was so surprised when the Matron asked me if I did it on purpose. What! I had no idea there was acid in the lamp or where it could have been. The GP came up straight away and said to the Matron that there was no way I could have opened this lamp, he had tried to do it himself and found it impossible. It took three months of being treated twice every day for the hole in my skin to show signs of improvement. Every time the dressings were changed, I was an object lesson to teach the staff what acid burns could do. I hated being on view like this, but I had to accept that this was a valuable experience for them. The lower part of my body healed, but even today I still have prominent scars left by this incident. A sad reminder of the past that cannot be taken away. All the lamps were collected from the hospital and one day as I was walking through the back of the hospital, where all the workmen had their huts, a usually jovial man who I got on well with stood outside his hut having a cigarette and looking absolutely fed up. I said, "Hello! You look fed up! What's the matter?" His reply was, "Some silly so and so got themselves burnt by these lamps. Have a look!" I looked inside his hut where every surface was covered by night lamps. "I have to check all these" he said. I exclaimed "Look! I am that silly so and so" and pulled back enough of my shoulder clothing for him to see the thick wadding of bandages. "You!" he gasped, "I am sorry Joyce I did not know it was you." I told him of the circumstances and when he examined all the lamps, another nine lamps were found to be leaking.

After this, the archaic-looking lamps were withdrawn from use.

5

The Long Winding Road

With the depression and living my life in a hospital, I had lost all trust in people. I became a closed person and my real feelings were my concern. But there was SOMEONE in my life who cared for me and who loved me unconditionally. And He was the King of Kings! He was the only One whom I could trust not to hurt me. I did not make a deliberate decision to cut people out of my life, but circumstances had brought me to the point where I had given up on them. From now on, it was just me and the Lord. It made my life less complicated. The staff still interfered by giving me treatments, at least that was how I saw it. As far as I was concerned no one humanly cared.

Years later, reading my medical notes confirmed many things that I thought at the time and revealed unexpected and disturbing facts. Through my own faith in God the most wonderful and positive thing that I can say is that my perseverance has proved everyone wrong and the medical notes to be rubbish. Now, years later, I have come through what every one said would be impossible. "Joyce will always need to live in a closely supervised community. She will never be able to achieve anything other than non-intellectual work, if at all. Joyce will never be able to live outside of the hospital." With this negativity from the staff and the notes, humanly speaking I did not stand a chance. Thank God for Jesus!

I never gave up in my prayers and though I did not sail through the heartaches of my life, I knew one day, yes one day, it was going to happen, I would be discharged, I was sure of this! I was surrounded by so many patients who had given up but I still wanted to leave and was still determined to leave. This was a problem for the staff as this was not the thing that patients did. By now I should have succumbed to the pressures and given up. One day when I was in the art department I painted a picture, I never painted usually, but today it was different. Inwardly I was declaring a promise to myself which I would achieve. I was given a big piece of paper and I painted it all black except for a small blob of yellow in the top right hand corner. I promised myself that one day this small yellow blob would completely obliterate the black. One day, my life would have the light back in it; all the blackness would be gone. When the staff asked me what it meant, I was not prepared to tell them. No one was going to rob me of this.

I was still suffering with depression and the treatment that was used very regularly was ECT (Electric Convulsive Therapy). In my opinion this is a barbaric treatment. A brief explanation of it is 'An electric current that is shot through your brain bringing a convulsive reaction.' A course of six was thought to be sufficient to help a person overcome depression. I still feel very strongly over the use of ECT in those days. It is used today but not so often and administered in a much more humane way. In 1993 a paper was published by Lawrence Stevens, J.D. and gives a history of ECT. It is backed up by doctors in England and America. The heading reads 'A Crime Against Humanity'. Here are some of the facts that I have discovered:-

1. "Electric shock therapy came into force in 1938 at the university of Rome. It involved 100-400 volts of electricity which produced a Grand-mal reaction. The most common usage of this electric shock lasted 0.5 to 5 seconds. It is looked at by some people as punitive, dehumanizing, brainwashing and memory destroying."

2. It is a fascinating fact that in the year AD 47 the Romans who suffered headaches were treated by using electric eels. Letting the eels cover the head they would produce shocks that could help with their headaches.

3. The first known non-convulsive treatment for mental illness was administered in 1755 by a French physician J.B. Leroy for Psychogenic blindness.

4. In 1756 one doctor in America having procured an apparatus on purpose then ordered persons to be gathered to be electrified. They had various different disorders. Some found immediate help, some gradual. The doctor who gave this treatment refuted there were any dangers while many others disagreed.

5. John Wesley, an English Evangelist, who founded Methodism, wrote in a journal in 1756 which was published in 1760. "Electricity was cheap, safe and successful for those who suffered from nervous cases of every kind."

6. In 1804 it was reported that two people who suffered melancholia, were helped by passing galvanic current through the brain.

7. In 1881, when children suffered from bed wetting, a wire electrode was attached to the children's private areas as it was said to strengthen that area and stop bed wetting. How barbaric!

I could go on with this but I want to refer to ECT from the year I was born, 1944. It was stated in many journals that ECT caused brain damage but it was said to be small. The press of the day belittled these concerns but it was a very big issue when others said there was proof of this. One paper said they considered the brain as the "temple of the mind", "the seat of the soul", "the greatest gift of God". "To decry any suggestion that a holy structure was tampered with, made shackles of medieval thought rise and difficult to shake off." No one can be exempt from suffering with mental illness in its various forms. Judy Garland, who gave joy to many in her films, had to undergo this treatment. She reported "After having ECT I had to return to the film set. I could not learn anything, I could not retain anything. I was just up there making strange noises. Here I was in the middle of a million dollar property, a million dollar wardrobe, with a million eyes looking at me. I was in a complete daze. I knew it, and everyone around me knew it." The studio soon suspended her from the film. In 1949 there were a number of reports of death from ECT patients in America. In April of 1950 there were reports of two deaths in England during ECT.

In 1951 an English psychiatrist stated:- "Shock therapy never builds, it only destroys and its work of destruction is beyond control. It is not new. The only thing new about it is the method of delivering the shock. 150 years ago a well recognised shock treatment method was to flog or frighten the patients, and with some of these ways the results were immediate. Now we do it "electrically" and we get about the same percentage of success, but some breaking of bones result and memory loss which the floggings never produced." The doctor continues:- "Memory loss in modern shock therapy may be passed off as infrequent, they cannot be limited and they are usually permanent. I have heard doctors laugh about them as they laugh about other things concerning mentally ill patients. The losses of memory are serious to the patients themselves. Along with such losses go changes in general intelligence and personality, but when these changes are too obvious to be overlooked they are ascribed to the mental illness with no mention of the treatment." This was written by a leading psychiatrist in 1951 and republished again in 1954. The doctor continues:- "This is a list of popular sayings said by the staff in 1956 and very offensive for those who suffer."

1. "Let's give him the works."
2. "Hit him with all we've got."
3. "Knock him out with ECT."
4. "Let's see if a few shocks will knock him out of it."
5. "Why don't you put him on the assembly line?"
6. "If he won't get better with one course, give him a double-size course now."
7. "Let's give her a mental spanking."

This was the way many people who were ill were talked about and talked to. I wonder if this is the reason why I cannot remember many years of my life before I entered the hospital. I used to be so terrified of this treatment. Although I had at least 300 treatments over twelve years, it made no difference to the depression. I had an injection to put me to sleep only to wake up seeing the next patient in the middle of having her treatment. With the terrible headache it gave me and the woozy feeling from the injection, I was off my bed and running from the ward. Today I can visualize the grey metal box; the dial to determine the voltage of electricity you were to have and the red light to show it was turned on. I remember that attached to this machine were antique looking head phones. They differed from the head phones we might be used to, because instead of ear pieces there were long flat metal strips with singed gauze on them. Those were placed on my head to administer the electric shock.

I am being quite blunt about this. It is something about which I feel very strongly. Although this may not go down well in some circles, I make no apology for saying that this archaic treatment should be permanently stopped! It originated in 47 AD, when electric eels were found to be a treatment. I do agree with this paper when it says it is 'a crime against humanity'. Let's get real. It is now 2010 and it is still being used, however it may be glossed up to look different! We are now in a society where modern technology determines how every one lives. What is needed is human beings to be able to listen and talk through problems with patients to ease the depression that is starting. The rat race of life today bypasses this and no one recognises the need "To listen." The only way I can bring any proportion to all this is by my faith, believing that every single challenge or experience I have in life is for a purpose and trying to learn from it. There are always more positives to be found than negatives in any given situation.

6
Treatments

Although I was not a diabetic, at one stage in hospital it was thought to be necessary to give me Insulin. It was, at the time, looked upon as another form of shock treatment. One doctor described it as being a 'chemical straitjacket.' A sister had to be in charge and only six patients could have the treatment at any one time. First thing every morning we would be taken to a small room where there were six beds. A doctor would come and give us the insulin injection. The dosage was increased each day and each time we would experience increasing perspiration and drowsiness. This continued over a period of weeks. At some stage patients were expected to fall into a coma. It was vital the sister was aware when this happened and for how long it lasted. The doctor would inject glucose to combat the coma and restore the patient back to consciousness. One day I was getting aware of the perspiration being more apparent. The sister did not see me slip into my first coma and by the time she noticed, I was in a deep coma. She could not bring me round and pressed the emergency button. According to the other five patients, the doctor and other medical staff came running into the room. The doctor was one who had a reputation for not being able to find patient's veins. I have no idea if she found mine at the first attempt, but I still have a blue mark on my arm today where the needle was inserted! Forty years on questions are still asked whenever I have to go for a blood test! I gradually began to come round. To help the process two nurses were instructed to walk me round the hospital grounds. It was winter time and I can remember them battling

51

against the fierce gale as they struggled to support me. I can still see the red lining of their navy blue cloaks blowing wildly as the wind caught them. After a while two more nurses took over. This went on for some hours. I was so groggy, I walked mechanically. All I wanted to do was to go back to sleep. When I eventually returned to the ward, I was watched very carefully until I finally regained full consciousness.

This was a wake up call to the staff. When later I researched this topic, I found that it was an experimental treatment of which the dangers were thought to be greater than the benefits. I was certainly not given any further treatment and cannot recall that it was used again at Tone Vale. Eventually it was discontinued by all hospitals. I had asked what this insulin treatment was supposed to do for me and the sister said it was to build me up mentally and physically. Physically I was built up, as I went from just 8 stone in weight to 15 stone. Looking and feeling grotesque by the sudden increase in weight did me no favours mentally. It did not help my depression.

This was not the only inappropriate way in which we were treated. The verbal onslaught to which we were subjected to daily was hard to cope with. Some of the staff would deliberately provoke the patients to react aggressively and out would come the needle to inject them. I was surrounded by people who had just given in, hopeless and expressionless, totally crushed by the system. Many times I had to give myself a good talking to in order to kick-start my hope. I believed then as I do now that it is not sufficient to just believe that God can answer prayer but that He will answer prayer. He has not let me down. It was as if I was holding on to the hem of His robe for dear life at times and did not intend to let go. In most institutions that were run in those days it was a common factor that staff would threaten patients with a certain ward. It was classed as the worst ward in the hospital and its reputation was well known. I was not rebellious, but I was always aware of the wrongs of those years and the suffering. I would often hear staff threatening patients "If you don't behave yourself, you'll be sent to Yeats!" Yeats ward, named after the poet became my worst nightmare. Over the years I had moved deeper into the system. If I was sent to Yeats, I would be lost for ever. My only crime was wanting to leave, to the point of being suicidal. I always knew I had capabilities that I had never been able to prove. The inevitable happened, I was sent to Yeats. I was twenty one years old and my worst fears were realised. The psychiatrist in charge was an ex-sergeant major and an alcoholic. An ambulance driver told me of the many occasions when they had returned him, on the quiet, to his hospital quarters after he had been found "legless" somewhere in Taunton.

Yeats ward was placed at the very back of the hospital. There were stone steps which went in a sort of circle leading to the locked door of the ward. Opposite the door was the Sister's room where the medication was given out. Nearby were the toilets and next to that was the massive bathroom, on its cold stone floor stood six large and ancient baths. On one side of each bath was a little stool where a nurse sat to watch the patient bathing. We had no privacy at all. The bedroom had big old beds that looked as though they had been there since the asylum was built in the 18th century. Beside the beds were little lockers where it was not possible to leave anything as patients, or some staff would steal from them. In the communal room larger and very old wooden lockers for essential clothing, divided our eating and sitting areas. Yet nothing was safe anywhere. The seats for our comfort were high backed plastic chairs. If there was a patient who had to stay in the chair, a sort of table was attached to it, so the patient could not move. There was no carpet anywhere just old wooden floorboards. We had yellow speckled Formica tables each with four chairs where we had our meals.

I remember that for the seven years on this ward I tried to survive on the thin slices of meat only, having found foreign bodies in the vegetables that the patients had to clean every day. It was the safest option! One side of this ward held the side rooms – that is a polite way of saying horse boxes. Put in a hospital at the age of thirteen, diagnosed with epilepsy, I ended up sharing a locked ward with murderers and deeply disturbed people. Some shouted all day long never making sense. Others smashed windows as a pastime. I was classed as a danger to myself because I had tried to kill myself. Every one of the patients on this ward had very serious problems.

The man in charge was hardly ever sober and perhaps had the biggest problem of all! I remember a day out in a coach, our holiday for that year, before we left the hospital he was totally out of it on cider. He came up the aisle of the coach with a tea towel over his head and a silver sick bowl on top of it. He bent over us with his long greasy hair and untidy grey moustache. The smell of cider on his breath was disgusting. He used his loud voice in a commanding way to make his presence felt.

This was the "doctor!" It is hard to use the word 'doctor' yet he had sole charge of my life and that was terrifying to put it mildly. He had the authority to do what he liked. When he was drunk or badly hung over from the night before, he seemed to take a sick sort of pleasure in degrading us. I had no respect for a person like that and he certainly had no respect for me. His expression would turn to sheer hate as he approached me. I must admit I did not feel at all happy when he was around, as I knew what he was like and I had to try and hold back what I really thought.

One of his pleasures, but for me a terrible thing, was at bath times once a week. We all dreaded this experience as we were made to line up totally naked. We were waiting for our turn for a bath. The humiliation as we tried to cover our bodies with our hands to preserve some decency, yet could not. The patients all had varying degrees of severe mental illness, all of us different shapes and sizes. It was much worse if you found yourself last in the queue of over thirty patients all waiting for a bath. It was always so important to me to get my clothes on. This was degrading and frightening, an experience giving me an idea of what a concentration camp experience could have been like. This was a worse horror than I could have imagined. It felt at times as though evil was let loose. I knew the only way out was for Jesus to step in. I increased my prayers and the intensity of them. I had to believe that Jesus would free me from all this. With new desperation, I cried out to Jesus "Please! I'm still here! Please help me!"

On Friday nights we were, on the doctors orders, given six laxatives each. We may not have needed any, but it was the rule he made. Every

Friday night after taking the laxatives it was a guaranteed fact that at least one person would be found on the floor in the toilet because she had fainted with the pain. It was something we came to expect. We were given our night sedation at 6.30 pm; this was so that many of the patients would be knocked out by the time the night staff came on duty. I was able to fight a lot of the effects of the medication but not always. One night I was awoken by another patient trying to strangle me. I had to struggle to get free from her grasp. After that, the last thing I wanted to do was to go to sleep, I always had to be prepared for something unexpected to happen at any time. It was part of the life I had. On another occasion, four patients went on a riot and smashed 52 panes of glass. The doctor would not have them replaced. Outside it was freezing, with very thick snow and fierce blizzards and now it was freezing inside as well. The windows that were broken were in the sleeping area. At night, patients tried to steal each other's bedding to keep warm. Recalling this now, I grin and shake my head in disbelief. Who could ever imagine this?

The doctor wrote to my parents and said I was too ill to ever leave hospital. My only illness, as he saw it, was my determination to leave. The letter had been written by a psychiatrist whose judgement had been clouded by alcohol. The only compliment I ever received from him, even though he said it in anger, was that I was "bloody-minded as I was never satisfied to stay in there." I was in my right mind from day one. He was right when he said I was never satisfied to stay in there. I was never going to give in to this regime and get sucked into this world. This is why he treated me so badly. The immense amounts of drugs caused lack of co-ordination. I reached out for something and I was not able to pick it up as it was not where I thought it was. I was so upset by life that seeing my parents did not help and many times my parents were asked not to come and this could be for months. It was a very well known fact that if I did not show I was happy, all privileges would be stopped on the doctor's orders. I have tried to remember what they were:-

- I was stopped from going to a cousin's wedding.

- When a big family occasion took place and some people were going to my parent's home I was stopped again. (I do not know what this occasion was.)

- The one and only friend who stood by me (according to my parents) was getting engaged and having a party. The hospital did not allow me to attend.

If these occasional things were my privileges I did not know. I wrote more and more poetry and had a folder of over 400 poems at one time. Some of them were personal to me and were never published. One day a social worker, that I did not know was coming, found me in a corner with my poetry, he asked if he could read one. The one he reached for was a personal one so I said I would rather he did not. I asked if he would leave them alone. He was a rare visitor but pleasant and I was trying to say "No" politely, yet in many circumstances you can be ignored. This was the case when he picked up this poem. It was called 'Three o'clock thought' because I had written it at that time in the morning. When the social worker read this poem, he looked at me and said: "Is this the way you feel Joyce?" The lines I remember from it, were :-

> *"Lord, please come and show yourself tonight, and let me know you are in sight,*
> *Please let me know that you are near so that I can sleep and need not fear,*
> *For I have sinned and kept you out because you see, I am in doubt*
> *If life is worth its wear and tear, So come to me if time to spare."*

The rest of the poem was how I needed peace in my mind. The social worker said that what I was writing down I should be sharing. I knew the impossibilities of this. If they had seen any mention of saying I needed peace of mind, the first thing the staff would have thought was that I going to take my life to get it. I told the social worker it was just poetry. He did not push the boundaries any more, especially having pushed them to read something private when I asked him not to. It should have made sense to him really. We were all in this place because we had no peace in our minds. It was very unlikely we would be able to find it here. We had been stripped of everything. I felt nothing more than a living skeleton. All I owned was a hospital number.

The Hong Kong flu pandemic started to take hold in 1968 and reached its peak in 1969, killing 700,000 people world-wide. Tone Vale did not escape its deadly clutches and patients and staff died. I saw porters carry out the dead from everywhere. I caught the virus too and remember being banked up in bed by numerous pillows. Every breath was an effort and my temperature soared. One night, I asked the night nurse on duty: "Please keep an eye on me tonight, I think I'm going to die."

She promised to watch over me but she had two wards to look after because another member of staff had died from the flu. I felt so weak but I knew I had to stay awake because I was convinced that I would not wake up again if I fell asleep. The night nurse never came to check on me that night. The next morning, the ward sister sent a patient with a cup of soup for me to drink. The patient could not wake me. The sister rushed to my bedside. I had stopped breathing. She tried to resuscitate me, pressing my chest in an attempt to get my heart beating, all the while shouting that she was not going to let me go. It worked. I started to breathe again. Later some patients told me what happened. I was only 24 and my life had now been saved three times.

7
Working For The Hospital

On the orders of the ex-sergeant major psychiatrist we were made to wear a uniform. I think he saw us as his own private army. What we did was called rehabilitation work. A more apt name would be 'slave labour'. Staff who were around in those days later confirmed this impression. Nurses who worked under him at the time complied with his demands, one wonders what they were thinking. Were they too afraid of him? Yeats ward was called a rehabilitation ward. Actually we had to do all the work no one else would do. One of our many tasks was working on the two farms. Our 'uniform' was heavy, ill-fitting navy gabardine macs, and wellington boots. It was a mad scramble each morning. Arms were flailing; the air was blue as we dived into the jumbled pile of boots, trying to find a fitting pair. Woe betide the unfortunate individual who was unsuccessful and had to spend the rest of the day in an 'odd pair', or in boots too large or too small! We had to wear our uniform even when the weather was scorching hot. It made sense when we were working on one of the two hospital farms. Each farm had different requirements. On the main farm we had to muck out the cowsheds. Our wellington boots were necessary for the sludge and muck. I had to milk the cows and it was not a job I would ever want to repeat.

On the subject of cows, John Wesley wrote, "Why does the cow look over the wall? She looks over the wall because she cannot see through it. That is what we must do with our problems look over and above them."

61

When the cow saw me approaching her with my three legged milking stool, was she looking over the wall to see if she could jump over it to escape my attempt to milk her? Did she see me as the problem, foreseeing the discomfort she was to endure as I attempted to relieve her of her milk? And was she imagining the inviting freedom on the other side? Come to think of it, I also longed to escape the pain I was made to endure. I could not be sure what was outside the walls that held me. The freedom whatever it might hold was so inviting.

Milking the goats was another nightmare! When we had finished, we had to exercise them on an extended rope. It was pay back time for the goats, as we raced uncontrollably behind them trying not to fall and get dragged along. Another job that we had to do was to clean out chicken sheds which were owned by a farmer about half a mile from the hospital. We had to walk up the main road in our gabardine macs and wellington boots with a nurse in front and a nurse behind us. I felt so degraded, as the people in the passing cars would all look at us. We had to pluck the feathers from the dead chickens. We had to clean out the huge sheds where hundreds of chickens were kept. We did it because we had to. From dead birds, clearing up the cow's dung, cleaning out chicken sheds, milking cows and goats, you can imagine the smell and the filth we had to endure.

On the smaller farm, there was a small shed where about twenty patients at a time would be set to work spinning and weaving wool from the farm animals. This shed was also home to a mynah bird. It had picked up some bad language over the years and swore at will! Usually mynah birds cause laughter, but when this bird was in full flow I saw patients assault each other because they could not distinguish if it was him or another patient! The cheeky bird preyed on their disturbed minds. We had to dig up potatoes. We had to climb ladders to pick apples.

I was also entrusted with other tasks. With one other patient, I used to go to the geriatric ward. We became experts in 'hospital corners' as we changed the soiled beds of the elderly patients, usually while the nurses were drinking tea in the office. I was the only patient to be entrusted with various catering jobs. Forty hungry workmen used to descend on the staff restaurant and needed to be served within the hour. I generally got on well with the workmen but now forty of them were calling "Joyce is my dinner ready?" "When is it coming Joyce?", "Have you ordered my meal yet Joyce?" With just one restaurant waitress and myself it was an hour that stretched every fibre of my being. Trying to remember who ordered what and who was first to order. Phew! The relief to see the room empty after the workmen left.

I was then promoted to serving the doctors in their rooms. The food was served in silver dishes that were kept in a heated trolley. I had to take the heated trolley along the corridor and plug it in. I set the table for seven or eight doctors in their dining room and then waited in the adjoining room. One doctor always arrived earlier than the others. He usually found me reading the Lancet magazine that was on their table. One time we had a good conversation over the Thalidomide problem that was prevalent at the time. I was encouraged to think that he spoke to me as an equal, though I found it intimidating to be in the presence of doctors. I felt ridiculous in my short black flared dress with a tiny frilly apron and the black and white band on my head. I was not used to silver dishes and fine food, and resented having to wait on people who had made my life so unbearable.

Later I worked in the hospital hairdressers. I enjoyed the atmosphere and became very accomplished in shampooing and setting the other patient's hair. On one occasion the assistant matron dropped in to tell the hairdresser that a new assistant would be starting. She saw me combing out a patient's hair. She was so impressed that she suggested I might go to college. The new hairdresser started. It was so sad to see how she block cut patient's hair, every one the same, making each of them look even more institutionalized. When the hairdresser in charge was not present the assistant kept decrying my efforts and the prospects of a college course, saying that I would never be able to do it. I was finding it so upsetting that I stopped going with no explanation. The main hairdresser wanted to know my reasons. I eventually told her.

The assistant was asked to leave for her 'asylum' hair cuts and her general unpleasant manner. I never did go to college but was asked to return to the hairdressers which I did for a while longer. Once a month I was asked to work in the finance office to check the monthly wage packets. The room was full of paid staff and we were all locked in the massive room while the money was being counted. One morning as I checked the amounts according to the pay slips, I found an extra £300.00 in a pay envelope. Having checked it several times I took it to the head of the office. He praised my efficiency as did a number of his colleagues. I felt so pleased and proud. It was a rare moment of feeling I was worth something. For all my hard work, I, along with the other patients, only received a paltry £2 a week.

8
The Way Of Life

Once, whilst I was recovering from the Hong Kong flu, which had very nearly killed me, I was resting on a high-backed plastic chair (the only seating available to us). The only other patient on the ward at the time was the one who had broken my nose. I had to have an operation to enable me to breathe properly again. My nose was never the prettiest of sights but this incident really put it out of joint for good in more ways than one.

The patient was deemed too dangerous to go out on 'rehabilitation work'. The ward sister was busy, with her back towards us. Somehow this other patient had escaped from her secure side room. She was approaching the sister with her hands stretched out in front of her. I knew instinctively that she intended to strangle her. I shouted to the sister and as she turned, the patient, a large woman, had her hands around her throat. I got out of my chair with a surge of strength that I never knew I had, and raced to the sister's aid. She had already fallen to the floor and I had to struggle like fury with the patient and finally managed to get her into the side room and turned the handle on the outside to lock it. The sister was still on the floor. Without saying anything I took her keys from her pocket and raced to the nearest ward to raise the alarm. All at once there were staff everywhere; the Matrons, the hospital management committee and the Sister's husband who worked in the cobbler's shop. The sister survived but her neck was very swollen and discoloured. Her husband took her home when she had recovered enough but she did not return to work for a while. When she did, she still could not tie the button up around the neck of her uniform. Not long after she had returned, she and her husband invited me to tea at their cottage. This was very unusual and special. I had a lovely tea and then the sister took a box out of a cupboard and handed it to me. It was a present from them both for saving her life. I opened it to find a pair of really modern looking black patent knee length boots. It was so kind.

The patient who attacked her was admitted to a secure mental hospital. This was my world for seven whole years and I fully believe this ward did far more damage to me than any other ward I had been on. Life had to be lived in such a way where anything could happen to you; always having to watch out if certain people pass you by, as if you were going to be hurt. I knew it would take a miracle to get me out of that place.

It was around this time that I taught myself to crochet by looking over the shoulder of an occupational therapist teaching other patients. One day I was told the Matron wanted to see me. What? The Matron wanting to see me in her office! For nearly 14 years this had never happened. I really did wonder what was happening and as I walked down the long corridor where her office was I pondered on what the reason may be as I knocked gingerly on the office door. This opened into the Assistant Matron's office. Then a cadet nurse led me through the Deputy Matron's office to the door of the Matron's office. The Matron looked very imposing, seated at a large desk which stood on a platform at the far end of the room. On the desk, instead of the paper-work one would expect, were two crochet hooks and some wool. She told me that she had heard I could crochet and she asked me to teach her. How could I say no? I was apprehensive, yet pleased to be asked to help such an important person. In the outside world this would have been a normal thing to do, helping someone in this way. I longed so much for the ordinary in my life. It was with pleasure that I helped her to crochet even though I tried hard to put it diplomatically when she did it wrong in the first place. I left her office knowing I had taught the Matron to crochet with confidence.

Another time that I was asked to help the staff, was when the Sister of the ward received a phone call from one of the Indian doctors. He and his colleague were returning to India and were wanting to film where they had worked at the hospital to show back home. He asked me to play the piano and sing. I played *"Forgotten Dreams,"* by Leroy Anderson. The song which was my favourite at that time was a war time song, "There will always be an England". I sang it with gusto as I reached the high notes. I also enjoyed the sentiments it had. It did not occur to me this may not be the right song to sing as it was to be played in front of the folk in India. Did the doctors leave the hospital because they had enough of England? Was there political unrest at that time between our countries? I laugh at this now, as I realised I did not think of the whole picture and this may not have been the song India wanted to hear. I did not hear of it causing another war so hopefully it was all right!

I received a letter from a friend called Phyllis who I knew in my Sunday school days. I had not seen or heard from this friend for years. She wrote to me from Erith in Kent. She was a Baptist deaconess and had a little mission church there. Out of the blue, she invited me to have a holiday with her. To receive the letter was lovely and yet at the same time I knew of the impossibilities as I remembered the letter saying that the rest of my life would have to be lived in this place. I did not respond straight away, as I could not see any point. I wrote to tell my friend I did not think it would be possible.

This bothered me inwardly as I had no peace to just give in and not accept the possibility of going. It would mean another battle with the doctor and I just felt tired of trying to battle with him. Simply to request anything was having to plead whilst he stood there with a sick grin on his face.

I questioned myself if I should try for this holiday or not raise my hopes up. Why did I have to battle for every little thing? I did not realise this was the first stage in the miracle I had been praying for, for such a long time. I realised some strength was returning and felt that I would never have another opportunity to experience a holiday according to the letter I had read. I feared him but I did sum up courage to ask him if I could go on the holiday. The inevitable answer of no came from him. I felt to use the tactics of it being my last holiday would perhaps give him the impression I would then give in and be content to live in this place of punishment.

After years of being surrounded by weird behaviour from patients and the staff, even that of doctors, I had learned from their behaviour. I gave him the impression of submission if I could have this one holiday. I am not proud of the tactics I used. I worked out how he would feel to think he had at long last won this victory over me. It did work to my own advantage and for getting the permission for my holiday. I was given a strict lecture that I would have to be back after two weeks. If I did not, then he told me of the repercussions and that I would be forced to return. I got the message very clearly. I went on holiday.

My friend lived in a block of flats that were several storeys high. It was a very strange feeling "to be out". It was so hard to feel part of this world outside. It was so frightening to see all the people below, as I looked from my friend's window. The freedom was terrifying, and I did not venture outside her flat in the first week.

I did not share about the letter at first but she realised there was something bothering me. She asked her senior minister to talk to me. I talked for the first time of some of the experiences I had been going through and of the letter saying of the life sentence ahead. To unload these things was so wonderful. It was through the sharing that I realised that though I had always believed in Christ, I had not prayed and committed my life to Him as my Saviour and become a Christian. The minister's soft Welsh accent and the massive load that lifted from my shoulders was so very special. I prayed to the Lord and an amazing and overwhelming peace came over every fibre of my being. I felt such peace and rest I nearly fell asleep. The minister who was sat beside me had to say the Amen at the end of the prayer for me. I knew that the Lord was present, and I also knew with even more certainty that the Lord had started to do something special. I wanted to be in on the action to see what He would do. The second week was so totally different. I sang in my friend's church for the blind club she held. I went on the back of her Lambretta scooter and sped along the busy roads with the wind blowing in my hair. If this was freedom, I wanted more! This brief taste of life was wonderful to experience, by gum it was good.

I had to come to terms with the fact that on the coming Saturday I had to return to the place I hated. The prospects that were ahead started to bother me, yet I had to go back and still believed in the Lord to continue His work to get me out of that place.

I now had my batteries recharged. I knew this was a taste of something far greater. It was tough to return up the stone steps to the locked door – nothing had altered. The noise and the havoc were very apparent. I had to think positively.

I had many questions racing through my mind; I had to think of the possibility that this place could be my home for the rest of my life. I looked at the way we were forced to live and realised we deserved better. The wards at the front of the hospital were painted and polished with ornaments and fish tanks and this was where the short term patients stayed. It was the part where the prominent people would visit.

I felt we were more entitled to have better living conditions because this had become our home, though none of us wanted it to be. The back of the hospital had not seen a coat of paint on anything since I had been there. The door which we had to use was broken where someone had kicked a hole in it years before. We were handed old televisions that other wards had discarded and had difficulty to watch a clear picture. I wrote to the monthly hospital magazine where my poetry of the Lord was usually sent. I had no idea this sort of article had to go through to the Matron's office first. Only when I saw an assistant Matron talking to the sister of the ward and looking in my direction did I wonder what was wrong. They called me over, and told me the article should have gone to them first but I genuinely did not know this. Looking back on this now, I am glad I made this mistake, as I doubted if it would have been taken notice of if I hadn't. In fact, as she was telling me of my mistake, she also said that the hospital management committee were meeting to discuss it. She was not a happy person.

The very next day as I went down the corridor it was full of painters in their white overalls. They were all spray-painting the miles of corridors at the back of the hospital. I did feel shocked, and a little guilty, especially when one painter who I knew well commented jokingly, "Hello Joyce, I think we got you to thank for this." He laughed , and I just said "Well, it keeps you in work. You should be grateful." I laughed as I said it, but I was tired of being the spokesman. No one could voice what they felt was wrong. The following day I noticed we had a brand new door that had been freshly painted. The biggest surprise of all was seeing two men struggling on to the ward holding a brand new television. One patient said, "You did this for us Joyce!" The sisters look of disapproval made me want to shrink into the plastic chair I was sitting on. The reality was there should have been no reason for an article to be written pointing this out, if we had been treated humanely.

Some patients never talked and became resigned to life inside the hospital. They had abandoned hope in every way possible. This regime had sucked them in completely, it was so sad to see. I could not allow this to happen to me. I heard from my friend again. She had heard of a Christian Rehabilitation Home opening in Tunbridge Wells and asked me if I would like to go. It was only the hopelessness I could see at first. I could not see this happening. I wrote and told her of the doctor and the utter impossibilities of him ever agreeing. Oh me of little faith. I could not recognise this was another step which the Lord was in control of. Four of the Christians, who wrote to my psychiatrist from Tunbridge Wells never gave up. I started to ask, again and again and again. This was so important, it was my life at stake now and some of my fear was taken away as I kept on asking him to let me go. He had letters more or less daily coming to him. His letters to the staff in Tunbridge Wells showed what he was like and this made the Christians write more. My life was made to be intolerable but somehow I kept the pressure on. I could not let this slip away from my grasp. This was about my freedom that I wanted for so long. I knew in my heart that something new was happening. The more anger he showed, the more he got out of control. He entered the ward like a tornado one morning, his anger was so apparent by his red face. He physically swung me around by my arm in his temper to a nearby office. He had totally lost it, and made unsavoury comments about these "so called Christians." I kept silent during his rage. I stood looking at him, calm on the outside. In utter frustration, he blurted out: "Oh, you can go, but you will be back." I heard every word he shouted out. I held on to the first words "you can go." I did not take on board the rest of his comment. I went out of the office where he still remained in his temper and I told the other patients that I was leaving. It was three months from reading his letter to say that my life would always have to be lived in the institution, to leaving. It was a miracle! A real gift from God!

The next thing I had to do was to get sponsored by Somerset County Council so I could live in the home in Tunbridge Wells. I wrote to them only to get a reply saying they never sponsored outside the Somerset area. I wrote again, and pointed out that it would be far cheaper to sponsor me outside of hospital for a period of time than have to pay for me to be kept in hospital for endless years. I am being totally honest when I say that I had no idea what I was talking about or even if it was to the right people. Yet I received a letter from a dear man, who said because of my letter sent to Somerset County Council, they had changed their policy and would sponsor people outside of their area. I thanked him so much and wrote occasionally to him to let him know of my progress. This was the last hurdle before I left, or so I thought. The day before I was to leave this doctor presented me with a form to sign. It was to say I was going against medical advice. WHAT!!!!! Had he forgotten he said I could go? I refused to sign this form. I knew that if anything did go wrong, I could be readmitted and sectioned. It would have meant I would have no say for a whole year if life did go wrong for me. Sections were used for any reason on anyone and I was not prepared to have this worry hanging over me especially after he said I could go. This doctor's hate was so incredible, but I had rights. I took them to the hospital management committee. I stated my case and they interviewed the doctor. He had to admit he said I could go. I won the case and there were no more hurdles.

That evening, there was a dance for the patients. The workmen who had painted the corridors played in the band. They asked if I could sing with them. The last song I sang in that place was Edelweiss from the *Sound of Music*. In the film, the song precedes the night that the Von

Trapp family escaped to freedom. I was leaving the next day to start my own Edelweiss experience of freedom. As I sang I watched the staff and patients in the ball room and my song was sung to them all as my final farewell.

9
Finding Myself On My Edelweiss Journey

The day had come! I said my goodbyes to all the other patients who had gathered on the landing. It was very emotional. I was so pleased to be leaving as I was the first patient to leave this ward in the seven years I was there. I remember so vividly how all the other patients were pleased for me. It was shown in so many different ways. How gracious of them. Inwardly I felt sad for them as I questioned how much more did they have to endure? The staff did not show any interest as I went out through the door.

I stood on the top of the steps at the entrance knowing I had made it at last. It felt as though this fresh beginning was like breathing the cleanest air I had ever been aware of. I always visualised this hospital as being constantly under a very dark cloud, which seemed to inhabit every crevice and every single corner of every ward. I was used to living in the darkness of despair. It was so different now!

I could breathe in the freshness of the new life I was going to have and the opportunity of living. The skies were so blue and I did not see a cloud anywhere. It was a very precious time as I soaked in the new beginning I prayed for. I looked up at the blue skies and said quietly "Thank you Jesus".

I was so grateful for the opportunity to start a new life. I needed a clean break from those in whom I had lost all trust, my parents, and those in the medical profession. I needed to get away from people who had branded me with the stigma of mental illness. At last, I would have the chance to prove myself. If there was a minor problem, which every one has from time to time, or if I felt down in myself, I would be put into hospital with no opportunity to get over it. I arranged to go straight to Tunbridge Wells without going back to Yeovil and my father took me. This was the beginning of my Edelweiss Journey. I was now seeing life from another angle as I journeyed to Royal Tunbridge Wells. I was so excited and then I was scared, then excited again and scared again. I had a smile on my face (because of how good life seemed to be) yet I hid it behind my hand. I was not use to sharing how I felt as I had kept so much locked inside me for so many years. I should have been able to be open with my happiness and perhaps shout out my joy, but years of being indoctrinated to be nothing and to show nothing had conditioned me to hide my feelings. Inside me I started to ask myself, "What will it be like when I get there? Is this the right thing to go away this far?" I had many emotions as I travelled; I noticed the skies remained blue, I saw the different villages, the different towns, wide expanses of land. I watched the sign posts as I always did when being driven anywhere. Yet, here I was approaching Royal Tunbridge Wells. WOW!!! I was feeling better and better as each mile passed. I had no regrets in leaving Somerset. It held bad memories and people there only judged me by what they thought they knew. The signpost said Tonbridge and it was now a few miles to Royal Tunbridge Wells and my new home 'Crossways Trust'.

I felt so excited and the butterflies in my stomach played havoc. It felt as though they were dancing around madly to the tune and timing of 'The Bluebell Polka'! – this was another piece of piano music I loved for the speed and joy when playing it.

The road was very easy to find with big houses on either side. Opposite the entrance of 'Crossways Trust' was an old folks home. It seemed a very select area. The driveway was curved and bordered by bushes. It seemed a long time before I glimpsed the front door but it was only a few seconds. A lady with a wonderful smile greeted us. I found out she was the wife of the minister in charge. She asked us into the lounge where we chatted over the famous English cup of tea. The minister was away that day but would be there the next. My father kept her talking and I can remember trying to stop him as she was a busy lady. I did not want anything to go wrong! When my father had left, I was shown my bedroom, which I shared with three other residents. I was not a patient but a resident and it felt good to earn this promotion. I realised it was only three months since I had read the doctor's letter which spelled out a life sentence in hospital.

It used to be a joke that wherever I went I took my handbag. Even if I went to the ladies my handbag was never out of my hand. Years of holding onto anything of value was still very much part of me.

It was a home filled with love. There were only a few residents when I first arrived. I was so thrilled with my new life that I wanted to share with someone. A name kept coming in to my mind of a woman on the ward I had just left. Her name was Bessie. I knew very little about her even though I shared a ward with her for seven years. I wrote to her. It was very unusual for patients to receive any letters or visitors. My letter to Bessie was sharing how wonderful my life was, how the Christians in Royal Tunbridge Wells and in the home I was staying in were so kind. I shared how Jesus was working in my life. Bessie wrote a three page letter to me all in one sentence. Her writing was very shaky, but the content was not. She asked me if she could go on her knees to pray. I wrote to Bessie and said "Yes Bessie, forget all the noise around you, and if you want to go on your knees to pray please do." Bessie did. As she was on her knees praying, a Christian nurse who had just started there saw her. She started talking to Bessie about the Lord, and then she invited Bessie to go outside of the hospital to her little church for weekly meetings. Bessie got permission to go. I received another letter from Bessie and I brimmed up in tears. The tears were tears of joy. Bessie had now left the hospital and had got married. It was so wonderful. Bessie had been left in the hospital for 30 years. Bessie shared with me her story of why she was admitted. Sadly Bessie's mother died suddenly. Three months later her father died. Bessie had a dog that got out of the garden and was knocked over and killed. Bessie was an only child and these three tragic events caused her to try and end her life. She was put into the hospital and was forgotten by everyone for thirty years. I was able to share with Bessie about my joy of Jesus now I had left hospital. Many others helped her and she lived until she was 82 years old. She lived in a bungalow near her church with her husband. She never had to return to the hospital again. I wrote to her showing her kindness and encouragement thirty years later. She should have had that thirty years before!

I can remember not long after being there I was sitting at the dinner table with the other residents and staff and we were all laughing over something (I cannot remember what.) I was laughing with everyone else and suddenly my laughter changed to uncontrollable crying. The residents seemed surprised, but the staff must have realised that the strain of my new life had become too much. It was a totally unexpected experience and quite frightening. The house was very big and being newly set up, the local churches provided many items for us. It seemed that every day furniture was arriving, and in a short while we had all we needed in every single way. It was so wonderful that it was hard to accept. I was use to a climate of despair; of no hope and feeling I could not trust anyone. It was hard for me to believe that anything or any one was genuine. To be loved, and to trust people who showed me love became one of my greatest inward battles. It had never been a part of my life and I had many of the old ways of thinking still in me. Yet, I did start to settle in and gradually attempted new things. I remember walking back to 'Crossways Trust' on my own, feeling so happy with my life and freedom. I started to realise how blessed I was. I was alone and to be alone was wonderful when all my previous life I had endless people all around me.

I longed to have a bedroom of my own, yet it was a blessing to share as I discovered one night when I had been there for just over two years. I woke up coughing and there was a strong smell of burning. I shouted out loudly to those I shared the bedroom with "Wake up! There is a fire." Everyone got up, we had no time for slippers or dressing gowns. Amidst the coughing I shouted "Hold on to each other's night-clothes!" We headed to the stairway. It was completely black as the electricity had blown and as we walked along the landing it was getting hotter and hotter and we were all coughing badly because of the smoke. We did not even know if we were doing the right thing as we had never had a fire drill, then other residents came into view and the three staff who were there at the time. It was two o'clock in the morning and the clock downstairs had melted at this time. Two fire engines were on the scene very quickly and I cried as I saw the windows exploding by the flames. This was my home burning down.

The staff took some of the residents on the lawn and tried to keep their minds occupied by singing choruses. It was not the best chorus they chose! I heard them singing "Give me oil in my lamp keep me burning." This made me cry even more as I watched my home being destroyed. This was one time I did not want to sing. The fire had started from a cigarette left to smoulder on a settee, in the room immediately under our bedroom. The floorboards under my bed were badly burnt. We spent the rest of the night in the old folk's home opposite. When it was safe to enter the building again, my room-mates and I had to sleep downstairs in the chapel. The incident made the head lines in the local paper and there was a photo of our ruined belongings being taken from the fire gutted wing of the house. It was an awful experience and it took a very long time for the house to be restored. Being in a small road, the other residents were awakened in the early hours. Hearing the singing and seeing the glow from the flames and the flashing lights of the fire engines, some thought the Lord had returned!

I had taken big steps in coming to Tunbridge Wells and I wondered what lay ahead now. No prayers went unanswered. I do not blame the Lord for the lost years in hospital. We all have free will and those in authority at that time made big mistakes with the free will they had. I was one of many who suffered. I recognised God's goodness in having enabled me to leave. It was at this time that, coming from the shops one day, I saw a friend in the distance. I raised my hand and waved vigorously to catch her eye. Unfortunately I used the hand in which I was holding the two yoghurts I had just purchased. They went flying through the air and smashed on to the bonnet of a parked car. I was so surprised and shocked at what I had done, but can remember how funny I thought it was to see the black shiny car bonnet splattered with apricot yoghurt! I was thankful that no one else was around to see what I had done, and I laughed all the way back to the Rehabilitation Home. This time there were no tears. This laughter was genuine!

I tried so hard, but I tried too hard. I pretended to be coping, yet I was not. I had a lot of joy and laughter yet inwardly the pressures of the world started to build up. When I was in hospital I dealt with everything on my own. Everybody who feels the need to pretend to cope finds they can only manage to keep up this charade for a certain length of time. I used to think that if I kept up this pretence for long enough it would come true. Sadly, it does not, and one collapses under the strain as exhaustion kicks in. Why do we feel we have to do it? It is trying to be accepted by people around us. It is also to prove to ourselves that we can cope and that we are the same as every one else. So we pretend, hoping everything will fall into place. I began to realise that all the damage of those hospital years went far deeper than I ever imagined it would. I had to admit I had been stripped of everything that makes a person whole. Where did I belong? I knew I did not belong in hospital and the outside world did not seem for me either! I had not realised how institutionalized I had become. I remember how hard I had to work to get out of hospital and now I had to work just as hard to stay out! I used to pray quietly to the Lord, asking Him to help me understand. It was such a vast world I was now living in. I thought when I left hospital that I would be able to live a normal life, but it was far from what I expected. I felt so small in a world that was too big for me. The resulting feelings of loneliness were unbearable at times. I now had to face up to new and daunting challenges.

The difficulty of being out of the hospital was like an unexpected boulder hitting me. I was suddenly filled with fear and started to worry that if I failed to keep going in every way, I would be re-admitted. I felt so scared as I tried to work every thing out myself. The more I tried the more anxious I became. For a long time when I walked into the town of Tunbridge Wells, I felt conspicuous. I felt that I was carrying an increasingly heavy placard around my neck saying "Joyce lived in a mental hospital for fifteen years" for the entire world to read. I now know that this was a wrong attitude, as if I was inflicting punishment on myself. I could not break this way of thinking. I was determined to fight this battle on my own, so I never shared my feelings with anyone. The problem continued to grow. It was so silly, there were people there to listen, but I could not get beyond the barrier that had been built over so many years. 'Crossways Trust' was set up and run by Christians. The minister, his wife and the staff worked very hard to provide a Christian environment in which people with mental health problems could be re-integrated into normal life.

In this Christian Rehabilitation Home we had to get used to working to set times so we could get accustomed to the routine of having a job in the real working world. One of the jobs we had was for an airline company, sorting the literature from the seat pockets. We had to sift through tariff cards, sick bags and safety information leaflets from previous flights, recycle those that were good and put complete sets into plastic bags to be used for a subsequent flight. Compared to the work at the hospital it was luxury. But it could be very unpleasant at times! I did not realise that so many people suffered from air sickness and remember thinking that holidays abroad might not be as wonderful as I had imagined!

My faith was encouraged as I already had experienced a wonderful answer to my prayers by being out of the hospital against all the odds. I often went into the chapel that was situated in the house and prayed quietly and also to thank God. This was also the place where I sang. Every year we had a service of thanksgiving for the home. I used to be asked to sing a solo at this service. It was lovely to sing again. At one of these services I was particularly nervous when singing as there were many more people there. As I was singing I stood in front of a table and the speakers sat behind me. I was totally unaware that as I was singing I was leaning against the table and as I did so I was gradually pulling off the tablecloth. The congregation saw what was happening but did not flicker an eyebrow while I was singing. It was afterwards when it was mentioned that the laughter took place. My joy to sing for the Lord in this way was wonderful to me and it also blessed other people. I felt everything I sang about Him. A congregation was present, but singing about Him and to Him was very precious. I was closest to Him in my singing. Because of this I have sung all over the country and in many different churches. I only felt confident when I was singing, as it felt it was the only thing I could do at this time. It still remains precious and something I never intend to stop. I was also asked to sing in our little chapel at the morning services in the rehabilitation home. It was a good way to start each day. There were times when a pianist was not available to play for the service and people knew I could play. If this was the case and a visiting minister was coming to take the service he would have prepared the hymns he wanted. I never wanted to play, as it did not come easy. I always wanted to say no but it felt worse if I had said no in these circumstances. It was amazing that every time this happened and I had to play the piano, if the music had lots of flats or sharps, I would sit on the piano stool and say, "Help" to Him above, put my fingers gingerly on the keys and manage to play the hymns successfully without spoiling anyone's worship.

The staff worked hard, and looked so tired at times trying to meet every need of the residents. I offered to help cook the breakfast for those who had started to work, so it would help the staff have a lie in. I had never been taught to cook; In fact I had never been taught how to do anything. I cooked the sausages, bacon and eggs and remember there was no talking, only concentration when chewing my cooking. The leather like bacon and bone hard sausages was a challenge for them. The breakfasts were hit and miss in their cooking, and after a while of trying to help out, the staff very diplomatically started to do the cooking again. No comments were made about my cooking, but in saying nothing, it told me loads. I could not cook!

One day there was an awful amount of work for the staff to do in the home. So I was asked to cook the dinner. I was cooking 80 fish fingers and several saucepans of food to accompany the fish fingers. Someone popped their head around the door and took a photo while I was so engrossed in this cooking lark. When I realised what was happening, I laughed and it was a genuine laugh.

I always wanted to work and when I lived at 'Crossways Trust' I got to know a Christian dentist in Tunbridge Wells. I went to help him for three months to see if I could do full days and regular hours. He was a wonderful man, and he started by letting me make appointments. I found meeting people in this way difficult. I did take my work seriously and wanted to prove to myself that work was possible for me to achieve. This to me was another step in proving I could cope with normal living. I then started to help in the dental surgery and was genuinely interested as I watched the orthodontic treatment being done. Then I was shown how to develop X-rays. The time came when everyone felt I could go in to the dark room on my own to develop two racks of twelve X-rays. I went in, and went through all the procedures necessary to get them developed. I came out feeling fairly confident that I had done a good job. It was now time for the dentist to inspect them; he went into the dark room. When he came out he just looked at me. It was a look that made me think "Oh dear. What have I done?" It was a case of what I had not done. I had forgotten to take off the coverings of the actual X-rays before I started! I went through all the procedures that followed it and yet the main one was the one I forgot. The other dental nurses said many people who did this for the first time also make this mistake. I am not sure if I believed this.

During those three months I was fortunate to be able to help a lovely man called Paul. He was deaf and dumb, yet he could let you know very clearly by his facial expressions, how he was feeling. His joy lit up his face and he had a wonderful smile. When he could not understand or if he was really fearful it was heartbreaking to see the anguish in his face. It was fear that stopped Paul from ever going to the dentist and he really did need treatment. It seemed that every tooth was in a bad condition. Working at the dentist and able to do some sign language I was able to encourage Paul to come with me for the treatment he needed. It took a while for him to come to this stage, so I promised him I would not leave his side. I kept that promise. The dentist was aware of the state of Paul's teeth and of his tremendous fear. He had already arranged for another dentist as well as himself to work on Paul's teeth while he was asleep. They worked quickly and the whole of the work that they needed to do was completed by the time Paul woke up. As he opened his eyes, he was momentary bewildered. Then his surprise expression showed "Is it all done?" I nodded yes, and that wonderful smile of joy lit his face up. It was a great moment for me as well to know he trusted me to be there and have this work done. It made everything so worth while. Future visits to the dentist were never a problem again for Paul. After the three months it was around Christmas time and all the staff went out for a meal. It was also a goodbye meal for me. I had made some good friends there. The dentist wrote the following for me to keep:- "Joyce, you can work. I have proved it. You have worked full days and I am very pleased with all that you have done." He then signed it.

During my time in Tunbridge Wells I used to sing a great many songs of an American gospel writer called Ross Minkler. Realising I was blessed with the gift of singing, I sent him a recording of my singing. He sent me a lovely letter and a contract to sing his songs. In those days an American recording contract was looked upon as a problem in this country. I had no idea of the obstacle. No recording studio wanted to have the responsibility of the money side of it, where a percentage of sales had to go to America. The problems seem to outweigh all I would have liked to accomplish with my singing. It was hard but I was truthfully going to be out of my depth as I was not used to the outside world in many ways. I would be going in to an area of the unknown. I knew very little about life anyway in the every day things, and so this wonderful opportunity did not come in to being. To have a recording contract was, I feel, an achievement. I can laugh at it now, as I might have only sold a half a dozen, so there would not have been many dollars involved. It was the right thing to do in the circumstances.

My worship was important, I started to go to a small free Baptist Church in the village of Pembury, five miles away from Tunbridge Wells. It took a couple of years after attending to decide on being baptised by full immersion. Being baptised in this way was for me an outward declaration of my commitment to Jesus, dying to the old Joyce and rising from the water a new person in Christ. I was saying "Joyce, your past is your past and now you are whole."

My fear of water was so great I decided to be baptised on a Thursday evening as I thought there would be less people present than there would have been on a Sunday. (I had not realised that having the service on a Thursday evening would have the opposite effect.) Instead of less people present than there should have been there were far more. The hall was packed. I sat there in my white gown and watched the endless stream of people arrive. I just had to giggle as my plans for a quiet baptism turned out totally the opposite. Because it was not on a Sunday people from many churches in and around Tunbridge Wells came to share this time with me. I had not thought of this! The pool was surrounded with flowers. The minister who ran 'Crossways' took the service. I decided to sing my testimony instead of speaking it. I sang "Each step I take the Saviour goes before me." Every word in the song was what I would have spoken. A lady who was well into her eighties and at the service wrote this poem:

ON THE EVE OF YOUR BAPTISM

This was a special eve for you
An eve so very dear
When each one of us with you
Felt His presence near
As you gave to us your witness
With your sweet clear voice
You sang of stepping nearer
You made my heart rejoice
As you went forth to baptism
You died to self and sin
You rose again victorious
A new life now within
As you stood in the water
A text was given to you
I know that you will cherish it
And it will see you through

As you go all the way with Him

Forget material things

Just lean on Him

For He is there

Shelter beneath His wings

And what a thrill of joy to know

That He is your dearest friend

He says "I'll never leave you"

Nor forsake you to the end.

This is what I have found all throughout my life. Although everything has seemed hard to bear at times, He has never forsaken me. I may have lost sight of Him but He never loses sight of me.

At 'Crossways' I had a bedroom at the top of the house. It was a little room of my own and it had been years since that had happened. One day when I was away for the day I found on my return all my music, all my bedding, and records covered in scouring powder. The room was in a terrible state, all my music and records damaged in this way was painful to see at first. I did not let it upset me too much. The man living opposite to me had a severe breakdown. I had lost a lot of my music, but this man had lost the peace in his mind. There was no doubt his loss was far worse.

The church I was attending knew I came from Crossways Trust yet never knew anything more. One Sunday morning I was asked to talk and I shared my story up until that time. Many were in tears, as they knew how the Lord had brought me through so much. In the congregation a couple were sitting at the back listening. Meeting them was a real blessing. It was still hard to adjust, and the thoughts of how naïve and stupid of me to think it was going to be plain sailing was on my mind a great deal. This couple would listen and give advice and it was with them I found out I had a great sense of humour.

My faith continued to grow and I met some wonderful people. The couple I met heard from the minister of the home I was in, that my life was in danger from a young girl who lived there. The danger often meant that I had to carry blankets and pillows in my arms in the dead of night to the safety of a caravan in the grounds. After they discussed it I was offered a home with them. It was wonderful to feel part of a family as they had two young girls who I loved very much and still do. I baby-sat for them and even though the girls could be mischievous at times, I loved every moment. When baby sitting, 'the girls' would use every item of furniture as acrobatic apparatus. I could not believe some of the antics they got up to! There were many laughs! I had the nickname of Jo! One day I was in their car and the husband was telling me he was going to be selling his car the next day. I listened and we bounced jokes off of each other as that was what we did. I was flabbergasted that as I opened my door on the passenger side the handle broke in two. It was not at a joint but the thickest part, in the middle of the handle. I looked at my friend. He looked at me. I was lost for words momentarily, and he said jokingly "Only you could do that Jo, I'm supposed to be selling this car tomorrow!" My silence turned to laugher, until I was doubled up. How did this happen? I will never know. I joked that at least 50 shillings should be taken off the asking price when selling it. The very old red mini was not worth a great deal but was handy to get around in even without a handle!

We still laugh, when we remember the funny moments of those years. If I filled hot water bottles for the family, no one could undo them. If I used a tap my grip was so strong that the taps had to be loosened by me as no one else could do it.

I remember when the oldest of the children was baptised I wrote a poem for her. She kept it on her wall for years. She recently gave the same poem to her friend who was being baptised over forty years later!

I remember how my sides were splitting as I tried not to laugh sitting in church one Sunday morning with my friend. Her dog had fleas and as we sat there a flea had jumped onto the coat of the lady in front of us. When it was pointed out to me I could not believe I was seeing this! I found it so hard to concentrate on the sermon when my friend and I had the flea hopping around in front of us.

After a while, we realised that it was not a practical long-term solution for me to live with the family, yet we remain good friends and still laugh at these times.

10
Growing In Faith

I am so thankful that I had heard of Jesus in my Sunday School days and as the time passes I know far more of how a broken life can be made whole. It is so essential for children to know about Jesus. They will not experience what I have experienced, yet other challenges can be there when they will need to know God's love. It gives a vital foundation for all ages. Having Jesus in my life every day gives me reassurance whatever that day holds. It means that I have the love he gives me; I have His Word to guide me in my times of doubt. I have the reassurances of His Promises with me every day. Faith is so simple. It is people that make it difficult.

My faith has been, and always will be, the most important factor in my life, knowing the Lord has saved my life. To know I have the King of Kings in my life means so much to me. One of my favourite readings from God's Word comes from the book of Romans, Chapter 5. It says:- *'Therefore, since we have been justified through faith we have peace with God through our Lord Jesus Christ, through whom we have gained access by grace in which we now stand. We rejoice in the hope of the Glory of God. Not only so, but we rejoice in our sufferings because we know that suffering produces perseverance, perseverance character and character hope. And hope does not disappoint us, because God has poured out His love into our hearts by the Holy Spirit whom He has given us.'*

These words mean so much to me as I have learnt a great deal about suffering. I wondered how or why I kept persevering, but it was a real gift from God. How did I know Jesus was aware of my heart as I shared all I did with Him? I did a study on the word 'heart' from the Bible. The word heart is mentioned over 800 times. It is described as a broken heart, clean heart, evil, hard, rejoicing heart, the secretive heart, discerning, submissive, faint, sorrowful, discouraged, trembling heart. It carries on to describe a grieving, proud, heavy, bitter, impatient, fretful, doubtful, fearful and weeping heart. This shows me without a doubt the Lord knows all about the way I can feel in every situation. He knows, whether I speak them aloud or remain silent, my longings, worries and concerns. He rejoices in my joys! He knows my heart and is ready to give the help that I need.

Many years ago I read an article that encouraged me, when I really needed it. It reads: "Complete victory over fear is possible in this life. Whatever is impossible with men, I can do. You can trust me with absolute abandon, in choosing the way that is contrary to fear. Making no exceptions, a life in which fear is resisted provides a better climate for victory over sin. Evil can do less havoc in such a life. In the same way, standing firm against sinful ways provides a better climate for the conquest of fear."

With help and support from gifted friends, I have been able to face and overcome my fears. They are not a problem any more. When my faith has been challenged and I am asked why I still believe there is a God after all I have been through, I say with all sincerity that although the forty six years that were taken from me were unimaginable, I have learnt such a lot from them. I am equipped to understand the awful torment of mental illness. I am able to use the experiences of those years in a positive way. I cannot forget them, but I do not let them affect me. All the experiences I have been through are behind me in a giant bin with a lid on. I only turn and remove that lid if one of those experiences can be used to help someone who is facing a similar situation. They are not part of my present day living. They are not dragging me down. They are no longer a burden. There is such a tremendous stigma attached to mental illness. It will only be when every one is open to each other's needs that there will be no need for me to talk about it. I can not yet see the day when I can stop lifting the lid to help those I can. It will be a wonderful day when people care for each other unconditionally. I pray very hard for this to take place. I know I have the Lord who can change man's impossibilities into His possibilities. I believe in this. It is so important.

The journey that my life has taken has been a time where, at every turn, there has been something to learn. At one time in my life when I was desperately trying to reach full health, I would grasp at any offer of help. Friends warned me that this could be a mistake. I found to my cost, that I had made wrong choices at times. Some of this 'help', even though it was supposedly in the Lord's name was not.

I have learned the value of advice from trusted Christian friends. At times I needed to know what the 'bit and bridle' experience was, to guide me back into the correct path. I made many mistakes in trying to find myself. People tended to judge me by these mistakes and many friends turned away. My faith has shown me the only One who will never turn His back on me and that is the Lord. He loves me. He does not judge or condemn me. No one person has all the answers to everything. We all make mistakes. I have tried to learn from these experiences. I have felt deep sadness when things have gone wrong and situations cannot be changed. If this happens I leave it in the Lord's hands. Doing this enables me to get on with my life. If you are dismissive of faith in the Lord, I suggest you find out for yourselves. I see my life like this, "I do not have problems now, I just have situations." Situations are easier to accept and easier to solve. With the blessings I have in my life and the blessings I see taking place in others, I want to shout out my joy at times!

It has been wonderful and encouraging to me personally as I have seen the Power of the Holy Spirit at work. There are very special times that remain clear in my heart. Blessing cannot always be put into the words because of its preciousness. Sometimes, today's English language lacks those special words you want to find. At the local church I was attending at one time, the minister asked a friend and myself to take part at an evening rally of all the local village churches. It was a praise service and my friend David was to play the guitar and I was to sing and testify. It was the beginning of something so wonderful, something I had never experienced before. The rally was held right out in the country because it was looked upon as the best venue for all the surrounding villages to attend easily. When we both arrived at the hall, there were many people already present. I did not know anyone there, and before we introduced ourselves to the minister we both sat down at the back and I quietly prayed to God for everything of myself to be taken away and for His words to be used as I spoke that evening. We introduced ourselves to the minister and we enjoyed the praise and worship from all who were present and I noticed a freedom of joy there. I sang my song while my friend played the guitar. I was then asked to speak. I have never had fear when I am talking about the Lord. I started to give my testimony of the years up to then. I spoke about the healing power of Christ. One particular healing was of severe migraines that plagued my life at one time. I was talking about God's love and suddenly noticed a lady had fallen to the floor with her face glowing, and talking in some form of language. I had no idea what was happening but carried on while the minister went to her. Two other ladies also fell gracefully to the floor and were talking in a strange language and their faces shone. I had not come across this before. Somehow, though bewildered, I still kept focussed on my testimony. The minister went up to the three ladies. On the left side of the hall a man came forward with a joy about him and said he had suffered from severe head pains for years. It had got so bad he was facing surgery. He said a real wave of heat entered his head and the constant pain he lived with had gone at that very moment. "I know the Lord has healed me tonight" he said. Throughout my time on the platform I had noticed a man standing by an open door at the back. This man suddenly moved from the door and ran up to the platform and spoke to all the people present. He was due to have open heart surgery but with joy and excitement in his voice, he told the congregation that he had experienced a heat and movement in his chest. The constant pain was gone and he claimed the Lord's healing that evening. I still did not know what was happening. I was aware something wonderful was taking place. I finished testifying about the Lord's goodness and went to the back of the hall and sat quietly praying, although inwardly I was in turmoil, excited and disturbed by what had happened. I had not heard about the Holy Spirit. The unknown language the ladies were talking was a gift of 'tongues' given to them by God. This can be for personal prayer or for the edification of the church when a person present can give an interpretation of the message that was given in tongues. I did not know this at the time. It was nearly eleven o'clock at night and my friend and I had a long drive home. The minister came up to us and thanked us both. He then said to me "It was your testimony that made all this happen." We both left.

On the journey home, neither of us spoke about what had taken place. It was not an awkward silence but we were both awe-struck. I had such an overwhelming sense of peace and of the presence of God. We went to our separate homes still without saying much. It was a wonderful silence that I had never forgotten. Unknown to me, David felt the same, and for both of us this continued for some time. He never said anything to anyone in detail and neither did I. Over a week later the minister of the rally phoned the minister of my church to say that it was confirmed that the two men were completely healed and their doctors said they had no need for their surgeries. This was the first that our minister had heard of what had happened at the rally. He shared it with our congregation and it built the church up and encouraged many others. Even today this still remains so very precious. I only speak of this experience if someone needs to know what the Power of God can do in their life. It confirmed to me that the Lord does not necessarily use the ones who show outwardly they are strong in the Lord or who can shout the loudest. He used me that evening. I was a no-hoper and a person to be locked away, to be shut out of the world of the 'normals' to which I never belonged. The Lord saw fit to use me even when I was weak. I was willing to be used, and I was. The Lord had answered my prayer as I spoke, to speak the words He would want me to speak. This is why these wonderful happenings took place that evening. It was not what I did, but what God did through me.

In my Christian life I have found it hard at times when I cannot be used by God because people only see my history and do not see me. I had a wonderful opportunity to prove my capability when the church I was attending was being rebuilt. I had just started to attend and a great deal had to be done in the preparation for the Open Day. I worked hard doing many little things, and the Pastor encouraged me all along the way. He saw me, the person, and not the label I carried around with me. I felt useful and I loved being relied on to do various jobs. It lifted my self-esteem and that was wonderful. The Pastor had arranged for an American speaker called Nicky Cruz to speak at the Octagon Theatre in Yeovil. Nicky Cruz was a very well known man who had turned his life around from being a gang member in the Bronx and doing some horrific things in his life. Now his new life and the change in him were so well known that many wanted to hear his testimony. I was asked to be responsible for the seating, the tickets, the money and making sure everyone who wanted a ticket would get one. My telephone number and address were made public for people to obtain tickets. It was a very busy time and also wonderful to be entrusted with this responsibility.

The day Nicky Cruz came to speak at the Octagon, I arrived early in case anyone else wanted a last minute ticket. The other churches were involved in the sale of his books and other Christian material. People were arriving constantly and I sat in the foyer with the remaining tickets.

A lady who sat beside me came from another church and she looked at me and said, "You must be proud of yourself getting all this arranged." I did not really understand why she had said this, and carried on selling more tickets. I had realised Nicky had started to speak and the others in the foyer gradually left to go in and listen to him. I waited a little longer and then collected the money together. I slipped in quietly at the back and I suddenly became aware of the hundreds of people who were present. It was only then did I understand what this lady had said in the foyer. I was the one responsible for all of these people sitting there. I had seen to their seating, their tickets and the collection of the money. It suddenly dawned on me what I had done and I felt a real sense of pride in this achievement. It was made possible because the Pastor, knowing I had difficulties, gave me an opportunity to prove I was not a useless person. He saw Joyce with potential and with ability. This was a wonderful help to me.

I had a great deal more to give when it would be necessary. Every job he gave me, I did with one hundred per cent. This is something I have never forgotten. It was also building my faith in Christ and I learned a great deal from the Pastor about putting Christianity into action. I did not just sit down on a seat every Sunday and listen and then leave as soon as the service ended. I wanted to be involved and I enjoyed every aspect of my Christian life. I was living in a flat-let, run by the mental health authority, with other people who had problems, This same Pastor realised I was ready to move on. The whole church and the Pastor prayed and helped in practical ways and I got my first real home. It was wonderful! This love and support brought me on in leaps and bounds. As I write this I have joy bubbling up inside me as I remember those times. There was so much laughter as the whole church worked together. I found my sense of humour.

I remember some particular moments. After the evening service we all had a cup of tea. One evening I was on the tea rota with another lady. We were both making endless cups of tea. One member who came to the hatch looked at his tea and commented that he could not drink it as "it was far too weak." I said without thinking, "Oh you like it with a bit of body in it, don't you," forgetting he was an undertaker! There were many people laughing at this and I had tears of laughter rolling down my cheeks. The Pastor came as we were all in floods of laughter and asked what was happening. Someone blurted out what had happened and he joined in the fun. He said he was going to give out a notice in church to come for a cup of tea after the service and a dose of laughter at the same time. I looked at him and said "We have made over forty cups of tea and had one thank you." "Not bad going is it?" There was a lot more laughter and everyone was bouncing jokes off each other.

I was given my most challenging opportunity when I was asked to take part in a Radio Four documentary on mental health issues, entitled 'In the Bin'. The producer visited me at my home and recorded an interview about my life in Tone Vale Hospital. Recalling many incidents from that time posed no problems. However, the following day she drove me to the hospital, asking me to express my feelings on revisiting my place of imprisonment. The site was in the process of being converted into luxury flats and I remember feeling real horror and incomprehension that families would want to live there. How could anyone ever be happy in a place that had witnessed such human suffering? My feeling to this day is that the whole place should have been razed to the ground.

The producer had arranged with the site manager for us to visit the church where I used to have my daily meetings with God. As we unlocked the door, there was a heavy, echoing, clanging sound, reminiscent of a horror movie. I could sense the emptiness before I even entered. The small pew by the wall mosaic just inside the door where I used to sit was still there. The rest of the pews were piled on top of each other at the far end of the church. The mosaic flooring was all chipped and broken and hardly anything remained of the old organ. I felt real sadness and a longing to see it restored, but knew I was powerless to do anything about it. As we left, I remarked, "I shall not be coming here again." I did not know until the producer arrived at my home that she had made the arrangement to visit the site of Tone Vale Hospital. Inwardly I felt scared and realised my need of God's protection.

In the book of Ephesians, Chapter 6 verses 10-19 it reads:-

'Finally, be strong in the Lord and in His mighty power. Put on the full armour of God so that you can take your stand against the devil's schemes. For our struggles are not against flesh and blood, but against the rulers, against the authorities, against the powers of this dark world and against the spiritual forces of evil in the heavenly realms. Therefore put on the full armour of God, so that when the day of evil comes you may be able to stand your ground. Stand firm then, with the belt of truth buckled around your waist, with the breastplate of righteousness in place and with your feet fitted with the readiness that comes from the gospel of peace. In addition to all this, take up the shield of faith, with

which you can extinguish all the flaming arrows of the evil one. Take the helmet of salvation and the sword of the Spirit which is the word of God. And pray in the Spirit on all occasions with all kinds of prayers and requests. With this in mind, be alert and always keep on praying for all the saints.'

Before the producer arrived that morning, I consciously 'put on the armour.' That is how I prepared myself to face the challenges of that day. It is God's equipment to protect us from Satan's strategies. The programme was aired and received an award for the best factual Radio 4 documentary of the year. A helpline number was given after the programme and many people contacted it both to express appreciation and to ask for help. The most important thing to me was that God enabled me to use my experience of suffering to contribute to helping others. I hope, too, that it helped people to a greater understanding of those who suffer mental illness, and went some way towards overcoming the stigma that still surrounds it.

11
Moving Towards Independence

In 1980, the difficulties I had experienced for so many years came to a head. I was living in Yeovil at the time and attending Penn House Day Hospital. One day I was aware that an important case conference was to take place. This was not unusual in itself except that, when I arrived that morning, the nurse assigned to my group told me that this conference concerned me. It seemed to go on for a long time! I was sitting in the lounge area with some of the other patients when my nurse, who had been sitting in on the conference, came and called me to one side. The doctor in charge at Penn House, who had also been working at Tone Vale during my time there, had asked her to come and tell me that the professionals present had concluded that I was a victim of medical neglect. My immediate response was, "Could I have that in writing?" I wanted proof for myself that I had not been mentally ill when I had been admitted to Tone Vale and that the cause of the depression, which had become my illness, was the fact that I had been left in hospital for too long. I wanted something to hang on my bedroom wall to remind me of who I was and what I had come through. The professionals apologised that they were unable to provide a written statement on the grounds that I might sue. I offered to sign any contract they might want to draw up to say that I did not want to make money out of it. The mere fact of their admission was beyond price to me. But to no avail.

It was after this that I found a wonderful consultant psychologist with whom I was eventually able to share everything for the first time. He helped me to rebuild my life, to replace all the layers that had been stripped away from me over so many years. He told me later that it took a year to trust him fully. At Penn House, an educational psychologist visited me to assess my intelligence. The tests took all morning and after they were finished he told me that I had above average intelligence. He mentioned my high score to the nurses and I felt a bit of a celebrity for the day. It made me happy to know that I had so much intelligence inside me. I was not a write-off after all! Reflecting on the years of my life, I am aware that not all the mistakes were on the part of others. I have made mistakes and hold many regrets. If I could have changed some events from the past, I would certainly have done so. There are some things that can never be altered for the good. The things I can change, I do. In many respects, my past has robbed me of the knowledge of how to live and cope with all the new situations that occur on a daily basis. This is not an excuse for having 'messed up' at times. It is so frustrating when I see how other people deal with the situations of their everyday lives when I feel that I am a raw beginner, looking silently on and longing to be at the same stage as they are. In saying this, I do not feel hard done by or sorry for myself. I have reasons to be proud of having overcome some enormous obstacles that the average person would never have to face. And I have done this on my own! I have tried to use all my experiences in a positive way

There are no 'ten easy steps' to freedom and not messing up after you are free. It is obvious that no-one who has been in an institution and had to face such horrendous situations every day would be equipped to face the world and leave behind the effects of those years as if they never existed. It can be just as hard to live in the real world as in the institution.

I have explained that I was living in a shared house connected with the mental health authority. It was not an ideal situation for me. Each of us had our own flatlet so that we could live independently. They were nicely designed and consisted of just one room. The bed was in one corner and nearby were two armchairs and a little table. The kitchen area, through an archway, was equipped with all essentials. The communal phone was in the hallway and was having to be monitored by the telephone company because we were receiving abusive phone calls from a disturbed resident who had recently left. There were other problems. Sometimes the necessary help was not available. I remember, on occasions, bathing an elderly resident. If she forgot to take her medication she would wander off, day or night, and I would sleep some nights on the floor inside her door to prevent this from happening. The situation was gradually getting worse and I did not want to continue living in this way.

My pastor, the one who had seen potential in me and encouraged me so much, was aware of the situation and the church was praying for me to get my own home. This would be my first real home and my first experience of living alone. I went to see my social worker who listened as I told him about the increasing problems and said that I did not want to continue living in this environment. He fully understood and told me that there was a clause in my contract saying that I could leave if I wanted to. I had lived there for five years so I applied to the council to move. I had no idea when anyone would come to take down the details. It was near the beginning of summer and I had washed all my summer clothes to freshen them up. As I ironed each item, I placed them on every available space so they would not get creased. I was very busy and clothes covered every piece of furniture, so I did not feel too pleased when my doorbell started to ring. I was in the swing of this job. I did not want to be interrupted as I really dislike ironing and knew that if I stopped, I would not want to finish it! Reluctantly, I went to the door to find it was a lady from the council who had come to take my details for council housing. She entered to find clothes covering the room. It was amazing that before I spoke, she looked round and remarked that I certainly needed a bigger place. I moved some clothes for her to sit down and minutes later I was on the council waiting list! How I thank God for the utter mess she found me in!

My Pastor sought advice in order to help me move as quickly as possible. One tip was to keep ringing the council. Never give up letting them know that you are waiting for a home. I did just that and was soon told of two houses in the same complex and quite near the homes of some friends so I went to have a look. There were ten houses in all. I walked up the path in the middle of them. One of the empty houses had two bedrooms. I had applied for a one-bedroom house, so dismissed it immediately and did not even look at it. I went up some steps and looked through the window of the one bedroom house. I decided that it would be suitable and phoned the council to say that I would like it. It was a blow when they told me that it had just been allocated to a young couple. I could not understand it. I felt so disappointed. Friends suggested that I apply for the two-bedroom house. I did not think for one moment that this would be allowed and could not believe my ears when I was told I could have it! A group of us went to look at the inside of the house. The rooms were so much bigger than the other house I had seen. There was much more cupboard space. The bedroom was spacious with still more cupboards and the bathroom was small but quite sufficient for my needs. I had a toilet up and down stairs! Every wall was painted pink and that made me laugh. If a man had seen it, he would have turned away at once!

This was it! This was going to be my home! I had no idea how I was going to furnish it, but I said, "Yes!" I had no idea of how to do anything like running a home of my own, yet I was not too worried about it. It was important to know the essentials, of course. This did not mean I wanted endless money in order to make it a show place.

I wanted a home and I was thrilled to have it. My social worker gave me a second-hand carpet. I had second-hand furniture in every room. In some cases it may have been third or fourth hand but none of that mattered. I had a wonderful home that to me was a palace. I gradually improved things. It took me a long time to get new furniture. I lived in my home for seventeen years. As I reflect on that time I have good memories of being there. But with everything in life, there comes a time when you realise that God has plans to move you on. Circumstances happened and I left knowing that things could only get better. I have not been disappointed. I have more joy and peace and a new life. Looking back I can see that it was another step in my journey.

I was reaching retiring age and I was still on a lot of medication. One day I seemed to look through the fog of the Tamazepam sleeping medication from the night before and begin to think in a new direction, one that I had not really visualised before. Only a few months earlier, I had been asking the medical profession where I would be transferred for help when I became a pensioner in the mental health system. Now I suddenly thought of being discharged. It had never been mentioned or suggested by anyone. It had never been part of my thinking, yet it was there. I thought, "Why should I have to put up with this to my dying day?" I thought of the medical neglect. The old mental health system had already been responsible for taking such a lot from me. As I sat in my home on my own I challenged myself. Was I going to let the mental health system take ALL my years from me, even when I was a pensioner? I had rising within myself genuine questions to which I wanted answers. At this time I had a lovely, down-to-earth community nurse who visited fortnightly. I had a wonderful social worker who had given me great support for twelve years. I had a real 'fun' support worker who used to take me shopping really early in the morning as I feared all that it entailed, especially at the checkout where she dealt with the money for me. I was fortunate in having a wonderful psychiatrist! In short I had a 'dream team' in place to help me. I realised that if I was going to leave the mental health system completely and say goodbye to them as a patient, there could not have been a better time to make it happen. I would act now and although I had fears, I had an even stronger determination to do it.

At my next visit to the psychiatrist, I had some important questions to be answered. Did she think I would ever be discharged completely? She looked at me and said, "Yes." I asked her when. To begin with she said it could be in the next five years. I did not want to hear that. That could have been never. I reminded her of all the years the mental health system had robbed me. She listened, knowing that I was telling the truth. I told her that my plan was to come off all medication and to be completely discharged by the time I was sixty. She said it would be tough but she never treated it as an impossibility. I started to take the helm as we worked out a plan between us. First I would come off the sleeping tablets. I was inwardly petrified at the thought of this as they had ruled my life for forty-six years. That would be the first hurdle dealt with. Then I would come off the daytime medication that I had also been taking for all those years. The third step would be to see how I would cope without medication, as the whole undertaking was massive. The psychiatrist said I might need to continue taking some medication during the day. I realised that it was important to listen to her. The plan completed, we set the date for the great discharge on my birthday in March.

I felt I would need extra help to achieve my goals, so I went to see Chris, who has kindly written in the front of my book. When I outlined my needs, his positive way of seeing the whole picture gave me reassurance. He offered to teach me how to relax when the stress took over and made sure that the doctor agreed before we began. As I went through the process, I was seeing Chris regularly, the community nurse was visiting me fortnightly, I was seeing the doctor weekly, and the social worker was keeping an eye on the whole situation. Over a period of time I came off the sleeping tablets, and within a week of discontinuing them I began, for the first time to discover what my sleep pattern was. With the sleeping tablets a thing of the past, I now wanted to tackle the daytime tablets. The nurses who were involved with me were very encouraging, though they may have been worried at times. As I gradually reduced the tablets, I was starting to feel emotions; it was as if I was coming back to life. I was on a daunting mission to meet

'Myself as I am' and it was hard work. It was extremely scary to come out of the fog caused by the medication, but I persevered. My doctor kept a close eye on the situation and as things began to work out as I had hoped I began to feel excited. It was a wonderful time as I began to stabilise without medication. I now had the confidence to go shopping alone, thanks to my support worker who had made it fun.

The doctor had said to me, "Joyce, whatever you put your mind to, you will accomplish it." Those words of encouragement gave me more hope than any other doctor had ever given. Originally I had aimed for discharge by my 60th birthday. But I now thought I could push my luck a bit further and aim for the beginning of the year rather than waiting for my birthday in March! It would be a New Year's gift to myself after forty-six years of struggle to achieve it. Knowing how well things were going, the whole team agreed that this would be a good time, so the date was set for January 19th. No one can imagine how good that felt! On that day I would be saying my farewells for good! When the time came for me to say goodbye to those in the medical profession who had been most involved with me, we sat in the office and talked together quite openly. I spoke seriously as I said that we all knew that the events of the past should never have happened, but explained that I held no bitterness.

They told me that people who have had to face situations like mine usually remain 'in the system' for the rest of their lives. They all agreed that my 'success story' was an encouragement to them and made their job seem worthwhile. I was so grateful to them and gave each of them a bouquet of silk flowers to say 'thank you'.

As I was leaving, other staff had come to say goodbye. Some had tears in their eyes and others looked really choked up. All had smiles on their faces. As I reached the door, a cheerful receptionist said, "I expect we shall see you around." And I replied laughingly, "You will not! When I go through those doors in a moment, I won't be coming back through them again. I'm retiring from the service!" I felt so wonderfully happy as I said my final goodbyes and walked home. Every step I took was as if I was floating on air and I had a beaming smile on my face all the way home. I could not stop smiling. It was a wonderful moment as I knew I had achieved my goal!

12
The Bittersweet Experience

I face my life in a very realistic way. I have experienced a great deal of unnecessary suffering and this is fact. I met hundreds of other people who have suffered as well. Some of them have needed to share their problems with me. Friends, friends of friends, even total strangers have come to my door. My door is never shut to those in need. I do not pretend to have all the answers but I do have the time to listen. The rat race of life seems to obliterate the important essential item and that is time for each other. All I can give is help, if I can, from my personal experiences. I have also learned from watching other people's struggles. When someone shares with me I can dip into the vast pot of my experiences and try to help and understand. Some people just need to unload the build up of pressure that is bursting inside them. That can be enough and it costs the National Health Service nothing. If someone has a specific crisis in their life that I can relate to through my personal experience, I can listen and tell them how I dealt with the same situation. I would always hope this might be enough to give them a stronger foundation on which they might perhaps build their own answers. I do not have any qualifications through taking endless exams, but I have learned in the school of experience. No special handbook exists that has all the answers. People need people. They do not want a page in a book to tell them what to do. We need some one to be there (free of charge), someone to care (free of charge), someone to listen and guide the person who needs it (free of charge). We need to bring people together, to care and support, to show love or give a hug, to bring comfort and hope. This is not impossible. You cannot get a hug by reading a page in a book.

In this day and age people race through their lives, so busy but not doing anything of value in their busyness. If only we could learn to stop, look and listen and be aware of the needs of those around us. Everyone will be better off and so would the National Health Service.

Am I bitter about the lost years? This is a question I get asked many times. I had never thought of it before, but after being asked this question many times. I decided to list the reasons why I should feel bitter:

● The permanent effect on my health of a throat haemorrhage due to negligence.

● The betrayal of being tricked into agreeing to enter a mental hospital.

● The feelings of rejection at being abandoned there.

● The shattering effect of broken promises.

● The pronouncements of worthlessness made over me.

● The resulting lack of self-esteem.

● Being made ill with depression as a result of hospital life.

- Memories of hospital life; the violence, the forced labour, the treatment I was forced to undergo, and the neglect.

- The loss of friends.

- The injustice of undeserved stigma.

- The total lack of preparation for the challenges of the outside world

- The lost opportunity of marriage and children

- Never having had the chance of paid employment.

- Living on benefits and not being able to afford holidays.

- Having very few memories of normal family life.

I cannot change the list above. I know I could add to it but I choose to move forward. I want to make the most of the years I have left. I can remember what I went through. I still tread carefully in certain areas. I know the hurts that arise in my thinking at times, but I rein them in. I leave the roots of it behind me as I know how bitterness can eat away at a person. It is a time waster. I have had so much time taken from me I am not allowing myself to be robbed of any more. This is my choice.

Perhaps with age comes a more positive outlook. I am proud to be called an 'old age pensioner' and I am proud to be called a positive person. The more positive I am, the better I am at turning negatives in to positives.

I intend to become a master at spotting blessings in disguise. Each blessing is like a prescription – the ones that do me good, unlike those I took in the past that stopped me from functioning. I can take this medication on a bad day. It delivers me from the abyss. You may feel you are in the deepest pit possible at this moment. My message to you is, "Never give up on yourself." Everyone has something special and important to give. Everyone has a special quality that stands out. I never thought I had a reason to be born, but I kept going. My motto became *"Expect the unexpected to happen, as it could be just around the corner, and expect it to be good"*. It could be for you.

13
Friends And Friendship

I wish that an outstanding new word could be added to the English dictionary that would be adequate to describe the wonderful friends I have. I had to learn what real friendship meant, as I had only been used to being snubbed and cast aside, so I am very fortunate to have many friends who have stood by me from the time when life was so bleak right up to my present joy.

As I try to put myself in their place, I can see that it would have been so easy for all of them to turn away as I went through the struggles of trying to find the life I was yearning for.

Over the years, from when I started to want a better way to live, many did turn away and this caused me a great deal of heartache. Sadly, some came under the guise of being friends but proved false, manipulating, deceiving and using me.

As I look at my life and remember those friends who stayed the course, I feel that I want to name them individually, but realise that this will be impossible. I could easily forget someone and I would not want to offend them. So I am writing about them without mentioning names. They will know who they are. Some have left a great impact on my life. Some have been there with a kind word or a smile at a crucial time and that is equally important to me.

Friends who are genuine are like precious gold. Such people have come into my life and I thank God so much for the safety of their friendship. I did not have to worry that they would hurt me or turn away. A secure friendship like that is healing, bringing reassurance where previously there has been no one to rely on. I can share everything with friends like this. It does not have to be about my needs. I do not have many needs now. We can just chat about everyday things and to talk and laugh about things happening in our lives is a very special medicine. We can share our joys, sorrows and worries and shed tears if need be. It is reassuring to know that if I am feeling like a talk, there are friends I can phone to have a good old 'natter'. And I am there for them, too, even if it is just to listen to them.

When I have important decisions to make, it is to true and trusted friends that I turn for advice. If I find myself in a new or difficult situation and am afraid I have got things wrong, I tell them what I have done and ask them if I have acted correctly. I ask them to be honest with me, and they are. I am grateful for their honesty and I can rest assured that they will keep confidences.

These often unexpected situations can be a real time of testing. I ride the storm and wait for the waves to calm down. My true friends are still there. They understand that the storm was hard to go through, but with their help I regain my strength and focus. I can venture forth again having learned from their good advice and trusting in what I believe to be right.

The practical help I have received leaves me speechless. There are no words to express the special gratitude I feel to the friends who have undertaken an immense list of jobs for me. I simply say with all the sincerity I hold in my heart, "A big and special thanks to you. I hope you will know who you are as you read this. Please accept my one million thanks because you realised my position and many times you offered help without me even asking for it."

Friendship is also about respecting each other. Most of my friends have families. It took me a while to understand that their lives and commitments were very different from my own. Yet in spite of their busyness, I was never shut out of their lives. In fact they allowed me to be part of their families.

All my friends' children are girls and I am 'Auntie Joyce' to quite a few of them. It is a real blessing when they give me a hug or blow me a kiss after a visit. Some are now grown up and married with children of their own. Some I remember babysitting and all these years later I still call them 'the girls', which always brings a laugh. It is unbelievable that they have grown up so quickly!

I had friends in the medical profession too, in the dedicated team who helped me to gain my independence. I must mention one by name, Mr Steve Denner (a consultant psychologist). Sadly he has now passed away. He had a smile that made his face light up and that in turn lit my face up. He was a unique human being who gave one hundred per cent of his time to helping others. He helped me for ten years, seeing me weekly for most of that time and then, much later, fortnightly. He spent time with me after working hours, trying to get me more involved with other people. I remember him coming out of working hours to see how I had decorated my home. In the years he worked with me, he helped me to learn to trust. That involved disclosing things I had never talked about before. As the time came to an end, we both decided that the ten years of notes that I had written were now unnecessary paperwork and could be destroyed. Of course, he kept the notes that were needed. We sat in his office with a paper shredder between us. The plan was for me to destroy the unwanted notes, but there were so many of them that we ended up doing it together. He looked at me and said how satisfying it was to get rid of the past knowing the improvement I had made. It was a great day. Without his help I would not have reached the stage that led to my complete healing. I will never forget him. He was truly professional, an excellent psychologist who loved his work. He was genuine. I was able to share everything with him. I could go into his office feeling that life could not be blacker, but leave feeling real happiness. Above all, he was a very good friend.

I have friends from all walks of life and I thank God for them all. To be a friend does not necessarily mean making huge sacrifices. Friends have cooked meals for me when I have been ill. Some were still strangers when they volunteered to walk my dog when I was confined to the house after an operation. Some have moved to another area but that does not mean that the friendship is over. I can still keep in contact. And I am doubly blessed when new friends come into my life. Every act of friendship is precious to me.

So, to all my friends from all walks of life I want to say, "Thank you for helping me to attain the joyous life I now have and above all for standing with me when my life was looked at as being hopeless. It shows what love and real friendship can do. Thank you."

14
GIFTS FROM ABOVE

The joy of the Lord is my Strength! Since my book was first published my life has been so full and I wanted to share an update with you. I have had the opportunity to speak to numerous groups and this has shown me the true extent of the needs that exist. Some stories are heart-breaking to hear, and for me – knowing that something I have shared from my own experiences has helped others – encourages me to continue.

I am asked to speak at many different types of events about the life I have had. Some of those meetings have time limits; others have specific themes to cover. These occasions are usually followed by a question-and-answer session, which can be very interesting, especially if there is a joker who asks questions that require me to be diplomatic; not always my strongest point! So timing my talk, and getting the theme covered can be a challenge at times.

I was once asked to give a talk that I felt was especially important to get 'correct'. There was no room for mistakes and my notes ended up several A4 sheets long. I needed to condense them and I started to remove different points but then found myself adding others. The notes grew longer instead of diminishing. Nothing was going as it should. The breakfast meeting was several miles away and as I waited for my lift I felt so frustrated with myself for not being able to get my talk as I thought it should be. I put the loose notes in a carrier bag where I had some bottled water and put it down beside me. There were many seagulls flying overhead and making such a noise, and as I waited my stomach was churning with the talk I was going to give. The seagulls were in full flow. Life felt quite a challenge!

Plop! This noise was too close for comfort and I knew something had landed close by. I looked around me…and realised a seagull must have been the cause. I could not see anything, but then realised my carrier bag showed some splatters on the outside. I opened it up carefully to see that a seagull had well and truly left its message all over my notes inside the carrier bag.

There was no way I could bring these notes out at a breakfast meeting! At any moment I would be leaving. No notes, only me! It was such a ridiculous situation I just had to laugh! Moments afterwards my lift arrived.

I simply had to speak from my heart that morning and my words just flowed. It taught me a great lesson. It showed me how God can use me just as I am to bring help and understanding to those who have needs. Over the years as I have stepped out in faith God has brought so much good from it. I marvel when I remember that talking to one person used to be a challenge. Now I have spoken in front of as many as 500 people. I even have shared on TV, as well as national & local radio.

I speak on a regular basis at the college in my home town. The students there have so much they want to know and I enjoy being able to help them in their studies. I had no schooling from the age of 13 years and yet now I am teaching students in the area of mental health!

I have learnt a great deal from life itself. I do not have all the answers falling into my lap; it takes working at. But my past no longer has a hold over my life, and if I have been able to help someone else because of those past experiences then it is my delight to do so.

I have a very happy life now!

NEVER GIVE UP!

Joyce Passmore

14
My Faith

When I started to believe in Jesus, I knew I was going to gain access to a life with a purpose to it. I believe in the Father, Son and Holy Spirit. He promised never to leave me or forsake me and He never has. With the proof of this, there comes other wonderful promises from His Word, which are equally wonderful and true. These verses are for each one of us.

God says:-

You may not know me, but I know everything about you...
Psalm 139 v 1

*I know when you sit down and when you rise up...*Psalm 139 v 2

*I am familiar with all your ways....*Psalm 139 v 3

Even the very hairs on your head are numbered...
Matthew 10 v 29-31

*For you were made in my image....*Genesis 1 v 27

*In me you live and move and have your being....*Acts 17 v 27

*For you are my offspring....*Acts 17 v 28

*I knew you even before you were conceived....*Jeremiah 1 v 4-5

*I chose you when I planned creation....*Ephesians 1 v 11-12

*You were not a mistake....*Psalm 139 v 15-16

*For all your days are written in my book....*Psalm 139 v 15-16

*I determined the exact time of your birth and where you should live...*Acts 17 v 26

*You were fearfully and wonderfully made....*Psalm 139 v 14

*I knit you together in your mother's womb....*Psalm 139 v 13

I am not distant or angry, but the complete expression of love... 1 John 4 v 16

*And it is my desire to lavish love on you....*1 John 3 v 1

*I offer you more than an earthly father...*Matthew 7 v 1

*For I am your perfect father...*Matthew 5 v 8

Every good gift that you receive comes from my hand... James 1 v 17

*I rejoice over you with singing....*Zephaniah 3 v 17

If you seek me with all your heart you will find me.... Deuteronomy 4 v 29

I am able to do more for you than you can possibly imagine... Ephesians 3 v 20

*For I am your greatest encourager....*2 Thessalonians 2 v 13

I am also your father who comforts you in your troubles...
2 Corinthians 1 v 3-4
When you are broken hearted I am close to you.....
Psalm 34 v 18

One day I will wipe every tear from your eyes....
Revelations 21 v 3-4

*For in Jesus my love for you is revealed....*John 17 v 26

*My question is, will you be my child?...*John 1 v 13

*I am waiting for you....*Luke 15 v 11-32

In saying yes to Jesus He came into my heart and changed my life. I love my life because Jesus made it a life fit to live. The pit I was once in does not exist any more. He has given me life in abundance and my hope and joy is found in Him alone. Jesus has helped me in a wonderful way. Yet it is just as precious and wonderful when someone realises their need of Jesus in their life and accepts Him as their Saviour without any dramatic events or wonderful healing taking place.

Jesus is there for everyone (as we are). By knowing Him my life has changed and He will change your life. If you are at a black time at present in your life, turn to the One who can give you the light back in your mind.